FROM THE CLUB TO THE CROSS

BERT ELDREDGE

Wild Ministries

From the Club to the Cross, by Bert Eldredge

Published by Wild Goose Ministries

Copyright © 2023

Editor: Shayne Mason Vincent, www.PastorShayne.com, Cover by Shayne Mason Vincent www.Canva.Com, Art by Deepsagar, www.Unsplash.com Interior Art by Harry Kasynov, www.Vecteezy.com

ISBN PRINT: 979-8-9870348-0-4 (1st Edition)

ISBN E-BOOK: 979-8-9870348-1-1

Printed in USA

1st Edition

CONTENTS

To my wife Kristie and my daughter Keshia, who went through all of this with me and still love me. To my sister Starla, who never stopped praying for me. To my brother Bobby, who still rides with me and loves me no matter what. To my Mom and Dad, who, had they read this book, would have shook their heads in wonder. To Charissa Smith, who took raw words and made them understandable to a normal non-outlaw person. To Scott Smith, who has helped with all the details in the aftermath. To my brother in Christ, Shayne for pushing it all to completion. I wouldn't be holding this book in my hands if God hadn't put it on your heart to use your gifts. And, my deepest gratitude and profound thanks is to You, my Lord Jesus Christ, who called out to me in the darkness and freed me from the tomb in which I was buried.

FOREWORD

By the strange circumstances of grace, God brought me to know Bert. It's always intriguing how little we know of a person's past until we actually hear it. His sister was one of my congregants and we met at one of their family functions.

As we shared our mutual love of motorcycles, we also discovered a mutual love for Jesus. This led to some long and profound conversations over a span of a few years where the Lord knit our hearts into the joy of Spiritual brotherhood.

As fate would have it, I had grown up with folks just like Bert. The difference being, I was on the receiving end of his lifestyle as a kid. Yet, through the goodness of the gospel, both Bert and I have been transformed and healed. I have a sort of life verse in 1 Samuel 2:8 where it says, *"He raises up the poor out of the dust, and lifts up the beggar from the dunghill, to set them among princes, and to make them inherit the throne of glory."*

The dunghill and the prince has actually been quite a literal experience for me. I was living in a city park when God came and found me. Through individuals of various faiths, God hit the reset button on my life, gave me a family, and an education. But, what truly blew me away is 20-years later, when my brother-in-law, who is a composer and conductor, invited my wife and I to a VIP event where we were seated with a prince and princess of Romania. While 1 Samuel 2:8 was a life verse for me, I never expected God to fulfill the text to the very letter!

And this is where God always has this quiet and beautiful way of weaving fate. It was during our getting to know one another that I had finally completed my own book on the Psalms, having taken me 5-years to complete. I was excited to give Bert a copy and wanted to hear his insights on it. It was during this time that he nonchalantly shared that he had a manuscript of his own he had never completed.

Apparently, God had laid it on Bert's heart that he needed to write his story down. He responded with, "Sure, I'll get right on that". But he let it sit year after year. I get it, writing a book is no simple task. I always get a kick out of the saying that goes, "Procrastinators unite... tomorrow."

And so God sent a tsunami of messengers to prod him. Friends would tell him. Churches would tell him. Prisons and jails he preached at would tell him. Strangers would tell him. Even emails from people he had never met. Everywhere he traveled, they all told him the same thing: "You need to write the book".

So, here we are and you're reading it. What you will read between these covers is how his hard-living outlaw motorcycle life was changed by an encounter with God.

Bert wasn't looking for God. And I wasn't looking for Him either. Yet in both of our lives, God was looking for us! And I suspect He will find you as well by the time you finish reading Bert's story. Because his story is about something impossible becoming real. Because no one is beyond being transformed by Jesus Christ.

-Pastor Shayne Mason Vincent, MSW

Author of, The Red Letter Psalms

Lord, make me an instrument of your love

Where there is hatred, let me sow peace

Where there is injury, let me grant pardon

Where there is doubt, let me show faith

Where there is darkness, let me bring the light

Where there is sadness, let me provide joy

Grant that I may not so much seek to be comforted, as to comfort

Not to find myself understood, but to understand

Not so much desire to be loved, but to show love

For it is in giving that we receive,

And it is in dying that we are born to eternal life.

-Prayer of St. Francis & Bert

CHAPTER 1

GROWING UP

Growing up in Wyoming, is different than growing up anywhere else. We have the strangest people. Cowboys, bikers, cowboy-bikers, hippies, oilfield-hands, coal-miners, farmers, ranchers, and drifters.

That certainly isn't an exhaustive list, but the breed here is a bit different. What's different about us is we all get along and hate each other at the same time. While we may not like the farmer or rancher that makes us pay to hunt on his land, we'll leap to his defense if someone is trying to take his land-lease.

The cowboy-biker may spend all day on horseback sorting cows, then drop his ponytail out of his cowboy hat, slide on to his Harley Davidson, and go for a ride. It's not uncommon to see a couple Harleys parked at a branding. That's how we pay for those hunting rights. You are going to wear at least two, if not four, hats on any given day.

We've got only around 500,000 people in a state that is 98,000 square miles of grasslands, mountain ranges, and wind. We work hard and play a little rougher than most. And I'm thankful I grew up here.

My hometown is an old frontier city called Casper, located right about in the middle of the state. Our little house was on the outskirts in a prairie called, Dempsey Acres. It had dirt roads, three junk yards, and a mix of the toughest kids you ever met in your life.

There were Native-Americans, Mexicans, half-Mexicans, and oh yeah, some ragtag Polish and German kids in there to boot. This is one of those Mayberry kind of places, where the furthest I moved as a kid was up the street two lots.

By government standards we were poor. My dad worked himself to the bone at the local refinery for most of my life. But in our neighborhood, that was just normal. No one really thought much of what anyone else had or didn't have. We all hunted for game to feed ourselves, we swapped eggs for milk, and the kids traded work in the junkyards to build our bicycles. It was a great life because we were alive and happy.

I remember our house being so small. I slept in a bed with my older brother, Lloyd, in the same room as my older sister and my little brother, Bobby, who slept in the other bed.

It was also normal to have extended family living with us. Mom or dad's family continually needed a place to stay for a month or two. I always thought we were rich because they had nothing, not even a house to live in, or food to eat.

. . .

MY EARLIEST MEMORY was when I was around three or four years old. I was playing in a giant mud puddle in front of our house, when suddenly I could hear my dad's truck coming up the road.

I ran and hid around the house about as good as a four year old can. I was covered head to toe in mud. I looked up and there was a very large man weighing two hundred and forty pounds, with a six foot frame.

My dad had wrists that measured ten inches around and twenty-one inch arms. To a four year old, he was massive!

Straight-away he had me by the arm, saying, "I told you to stay out of that puddle!"

Instantly, my sixty pound sister Starla flew between me and him. She was right up in my dad's business, "Let him be! I'll clean him up!"

This was one of the thousand times my older sister saved my life. At the time, my dad seemed mad to me, but when he tells the story he was not mad at all. He laughs, "The only thing white on you were your eyes looking up at me!"

Certainly my dad gave us spankings, but never beatings; we were the Eldredge boys, believe me, we had each one of them coming, and didn't get half of what we should have.

CHAPTER 2
LITTLE-LLOYD

My older brother, Lloyd, my father's name sake, was eleven years older than me, and I looked up to him and tried to act like him.

While he was never a big person, small as far as the Eldredge clan goes. He was maybe a hundred and sixty pounds, thin framed, with dark curly hair and dark skin.

I wanted curly hair just like his! Lloyd used to wear a blue welders hat with white polka dots all over it. He had me convinced it was what made his hair curly.

One day, I was looking in the mirror watching as he was combing his hair.

He said "You know what little bud? I got something for ya."

He pulled out a little blue welders hat and put it on my head. Lloyd had someone make it for me just like his with white polka dots.

I slept with that dang thing on. It never left my sight.

Mom would fight it off my head to give me a bath.

I ADORED LITTLE-LLOYD, he could do no wrong in my eyes. And he was the one who introduced me to motorcycles.

I can almost hear the straight pipes on the Royal Enfield Twin as he pulled it into the yard for the first time. I also remember my dad's face, believing my brother had spent good money on what he obviously saw as a pile of junk. A long chrome front end and a tall old sissy bar with a king-queen seat on the back.

My heart stood still as a thrill ran through my bones. Over the next few days, he had that bike so shiny and clean he didn't even need a light at night. I still get that same feeling when I see a really cool chopper.

By my first ride down the old dirt road, I was hooked. And I would put up a fight every time someone else had a turn.

My little brother Bobby and I rode daily, or at least every time Lloyd would let us. Man, the wind in your face, the crack of the throttle making those pipes sing, it was a stone cold addiction!

One time, he woke me up about 3 AM, "You wanna go for a putt and see the sunrise?" Like a shot, I was up and dressed as fast as could be. We fired up the bike, he slipped my helmet on and I crawled on the back seat. The air was so cold I could hardly breathe.

I buried my face in his back and took a deep breath.

We rode all over that night, ending up at a truck-stop having coffee and hot chocolate. Just before the sunrise, he paid the lady saying, "We need to hustle little man, you don't want to miss this!"

The sun rose just like it did any other day, but this moment was different for me and I knew it. The only sound was the pipes singing, a tune that filled the air with life as the sun broke over the horizon. It seemed to ignite the grass with color.

It was the greatest moment of my eight year old life. It was also the very last ride I would ever take with my brother.

TWO MONTHS LATER, I woke up as someone was placing me in my parent's bed. Several people were crying in the other room. Presently they brought in my little brother who I woke up, saying, "Something is wrong, dad's home"; my dad normally worked nights at the refinery.

I started to get out of bed when my mom came in the room.

She hugged me and Bobby tightly. I was scared because I had never seen my mom cry, she was a pretty tough lady. Mom said, "Something bad has happened..."

I wanted to know what, but she was crying so hard I thought she couldn't talk. I started patting her on the shoulder and Bobby copied me.

"Your brother was in an accident..." the words came out in a sob.

"Well, have the doctors put a band-aid on him and bring him home!" Bobby said.

My mom cried even harder. I didn't know what was wrong, but I knew I was scared and I could feel in my soul something was not right. "Your brother is dead."

I didn't cry, I didn't shake, I went numb. "Dead?" What does dead mean? Why is he dead? Where is he? Why is everyone crying? What does this mean?

I got out of bed and went to the front yard where I could hear my dad crying.

Shattered does not begin to explain what I saw in my dad's face. He was leaning against a small tree and openly sobbing.

My dad looked up into the sky, "Why have you taken my boy?! Why have you taken my son from me? Dear God, why have you done this?"

I looked to the sky myself and looked back at dad. My heart sank because I knew this was not a dream, this was now very real.

I knew who God was, that He was all powerful and in control of all things. He took my brother? Why? What did we do to Him? We prayed at every meal, my dad didn't break any of His rules. Why did God hate us?

My mind sat and spun for a minute. My heart filled with hurt and confusion, my fists clenched tight at my side, my eyes filling with tears. "You took my brother," I whispered under my breath. "You hate me," slipped through my clenched teeth. I looked up and said, "I hate You!"

My dad heard me and grabbed me up. He squeezed me so hard I thought I would burst. "My boy, my boy, my boy," he just kept saying.

. . .

LITTLE-LLOYD HAD BEEN RIDING up Casper Mountain with a couple of friends. One friend had stopped for fuel, but my brother kept going.

As Lloyd headed up the mountain to a party, another guy with two girls had left that same party. He was drunk and driving so fast he lost control of the car, it went sideways and slid more than one-hundred feet before slamming into my brother's motorcycle.

Lloyd died instantly. The girl riding on the back of his motorcycle and the girl in the back seat of the car were also killed.

And the man that hit my brother? He never saw the inside of jail. While he was never in prison, he spent the rest of his days in hell because he never forgave himself.

Many lives were destroyed in the blink of an eye that day. Not just those in the the accident. And this was the turning point of my own life, where anger at God led to my own personal hell.

CHAPTER 3
LET THE MISCHIEF BEGIN

I was only 9 years old when I helped with my first break in. Granted, it was a bit comical. But it was still wrong.

I was the lookout for some older boys while they went in to rob the house. They took important things like baloney, beer, and smokes.

Money? We were kids with no concept of money, it really had no meaning for us. But I'd never tasted beer, nor had I ever had a smell of smoke. My folks didn't do that kind of stuff. But these kids? Their parents were hard core.

As we headed out to divide up the loot in our junkyard hangout, one of their sisters spotted us. The older boys had an argument with her, so we split the two beers and baloney and prepared to run.

The older boys laid claim to the smokes, but gave me and one of my buddies each a drink of beer. It was the worst tasting crap I had ever put in my mouth! So I took a second drink.

When I finally got home that afternoon, I made sure my teeth were brushed. Not to cover the beer smell, but because puke tastes bad! Too much baloney and beer mixed in a nine year old body; yeah, you knew it would happen.

LATER THAT DAY, I heard a car drive up and my mom was outside. I saw the mom of the boys down the street talking to my mom. When they both turned and looked at the house, I knew I was about to die.

Was my mom going to beat me slowly and turn the screws? Or was she going to wait until dad got home and I'd die in a blinding flash of "fists of fury"? Ah, the nine year old's mind. Everything was a bit of a blur for a few hours.

Dad did come home and question me. But he didn't beat me or yell. He did asked me who I was with. "I can't remember" was my mumbled response.

"Well, your buddy's mom already told me", raising his eyebrow.

I looked him square in the eye, "If she told you, why you askin' me?"

That response got a little flair of temper.

"Boy, you're going to tell me who was with you." His tone had trouble written all over it.

I took a deep breath and tightened my butt cheeks, "I don't remember."

Switching tactics, he demanded, "Then what did you take?" "Nothing." "What did they take?" "It wasn't my doing, I'm not sure."

By the time the interrogation was over, my dad had to leave the room and compose himself so he didn't kill me. I wasn't going to rat anyone out and that was that!

AFTER WHAT SEEMED LIKE HOURS, my dad came back in the room and loaded me in the car. We were headed to the house that was broken into.

The man who owned the house was named Chick; he owned the biggest junkyard in our neighborhood. I was dreading how this was going to shake out when Chick met my dad at the door.

The two of them talked for a bit. Then it was my turn.

Chick looked down at me and asked, "So, what did you take?" "Some food and some beer" "Did you take it or did someone else take it?"

I looked at my dad and looked back at Chick, "I took it."

They both knew there were more people involved, they wanted to ask, but it was obvious I wasn't going to tell.

Chick said, "Little outlaw are we? Well, a thief has got no place in this world and no friends. Your dad is my friend and I am going to let him choose how to punish you out of respect for him."

Those words hit me pretty hard. I knew that he respected my dad and was not at all impressed with me.

Chick was an old school Polish guy, so he never considered calling the cops. And it was obvious to me that he didn't even know the stuff was missing.

My dad ended it, "I'll make it right with you Chick." So, he sent me back to sort bolts in the shed until the cost of baloney and two beers was paid in full.

That was certainly one full Saturday.

LATER ON, Chick sat me down in his shop and said, "You're going to amount to something because you didn't blame anyone else for your actions. While the other older boys took their beatings, they never came and talked with me. You have more courage than those other boys because you paid your debt. Your father is an honorable man. You should be like him, not an outlaw."

I heard him for the moment, but it didn't last.

By 10 years old, I shoplifted my first Iron Horse magazine. The only reason I got Iron Horse was because I couldn't reach the Easyrider.

I brought it to school the next day and all of the kids were staring at the half naked girls in the book. But I looked right past them to the beautiful chrome and black choppers and decided right then and there, I was going to be a biker!

CHAPTER 4
THE AMIGOS

From that moment on, my best-buds and I, Steve, Marvin, and Lance, were always into some kind of mischief. We were together all day every day, and what one didn't think of, the others did.

We all built our life around motorcycles: bicycles, mini-bikes, dirt bikes, whatever had two wheels and hauled-butt.

But with Little-Loyd's history, my dad made my younger brother and I promise to not get street bikes until we were eighteen. Basically the speech was, "As long as you're under my roof, you won't be riding on the street!" You can imagine how that went. I couldn't stay away from bikes!

When I got a bit older, I would sneak over to my buddies' place where he had a 1969 Sportster. What a bike! When I think back on it now I am amazed at how God kept us alive on that stupid thing.

One day, we were out jumping ditches with it, I guess we were trying to be Steve Macqueen or something, and broke the rod that ran to the mechanical brakes. So, we found a deer leg-bone in a fence and bailing wired it to the swing-arm and the rod to the leg.

It now took two people to ride the bike. One to run the bike and the one on back to press down on the bone to slow it down, then we would both drag our feet. I know what you're thinking genius, right? I know, we were super smart.

Once, when we were only eleven or twelve, we stole Steve's brother's car and cruised our hood. We ran the dang thing out of gas down by my sister's house.

We were too dumb to know we were out of gas, so we cranked it until it was dead. In fear for our lives, we tried to push start it, and just about that time, Steve's mom came down the road.

We got the gas and a jump alright, but we also got our butts whipped!

Steve and Marvin's families were Catholic, so for the rest of our punishment we ended up helping some nuns move. While the priests were cool, the nuns were not.

DURING THAT SUMMER, one of the guys had a bunch of bulls from the rodeo in their corrals.

All of about a dozen of us kids stared at the size of those bulls and a plan began to form.

The family that owned the pens had a practice chute, so we herded those bulls into the ones that were used for high school rodeo practice.

Now it just so happened that Little-Lloyd had been an avid rodeo rider, and had left me his bull riding rope; so, when they asked, "Who's gonna go first?" I stepped right up.

This was another chance to emulate my big-brother and I wasn't going to miss it!

So, with some finagling, we figured out how to put the rigging on and I loaded up. Everyone got ready and I hollered, "Let 'er buck, boys"! The gate flew open. I was ready to go flying through the air... but the bull just stood there. Finally it lumbered out of the gate.

I banged on his sides with my feet and he finally gave me a couple of little bucks. He gave me a good shake and knocked me off. Disappointed, we all had a talk. We figured out that usually there is a cinch belt on the bull and they hit it with a cattle prod. We were able to get a prod, but not a cinch.

STEVE WAS NEXT, when the gate flew open, someone hit the bull with the prod.

The first jump looked to me like it was five feet in the air and the bull was pissed. Steve, on the other hand, flew much higher than the bull, reaching new heights of understanding of why kids should not ride rodeo bulls.

When he finally came down in a cloud of dust and a large grunt, the bull was off running, with the dang rigging still around him. This took us a little while to retrieve. The bull was irritated, and ran us up and over the fence a few times before we got our stuff back. Stupid bull!

. . .

NEXT WAS A KID NAMED CHAD. Chad was a sensitive kid, he was older than us, but soft. We convinced him that this is what it took to fit into our little posse.

He went in the chute on the bull almost crying. Marvin rolling his eyes yelled, "Suck it up".

I had the prod this time and just as they were pulling the chute gate, I hit that bull square in the balls. Man alive did he buck!

I don't think Chad made the eight seconds, in fact I am sure it was about the third jump straight into the air that we saw Chad come off.

There was one little issue, Chad was caught in the rigging. The bull shook Chad into a pile of tears, blood running from his nose, his hand slightly blue and his face too.

IT WAS about this time that my dad crested the hill coming home from mornings at the refinery. He was less than pleased and I am pretty sure none of us could sit down for a week when word got out that we had decided to be rodeo stars.

You gotta understand, during the day in our neighborhood all parents worked and we pretty much had a "Lord of the flies" thing happening out there.

The older kids were supposed to keep an eye on the younger kids. And after the bull riding incident, the older kids tried to keep better tabs on us. This led to us discovering all kinds of stuff. Stuff we should not have known for many more years.

ONE YEAR, my dad built us a baseball diamond. That diamond became something that kept us occupied for days.

We lived in upper Dempsey and there were kids just over the hill in lower Dempsey. We always thought they were rich kids. Trust me, they weren't. We would challenge them every Friday to a game of baseball. It was a great couple of summers doing that.

In fact, that is where I learned how to be a true leader.

One time, I was in trouble and my dad told me I had to paint the fence as punishment. Soon after, Steven and Marvin were at the house and wanted to go play ball.

"I can't until the fence is done," I told them.

So, they began to help; then other kids from the neighborhood showed up, and they were all painting the fence. Even kids from lower Dempsey showed up and helped.

All of the sudden, my dad was standing next to me, "Who are all these kids?" "They wanna play ball. So, I told them we need to get this work done first before I can play."

He studied the group of kids carefully before asking me, "Why are they all covered in paint and you don't have any paint on you?" "Dad, someone has to be the boss," I said, not even looking up at him.

When he told the story later, he always said, "Bert was born to lead. It just seemed to be his calling in life".

INEVITABLY, I began to experiment with drugs and alcohol. It all started while we were playing in the junkyard. One of the older boys offered me some "rush".

"What is 'rush'?" I said cocking my head. "Record cleaner", he told me.

He opened the little bottle and took about four or five deep breaths. His eyes rolled back as he laid back on the hood of a car.

"Try it", he told me, "It'll give you a buzz." So, I took about three whiffs of it. My eyes felt like they were going to blow up and my ears were buzzing. We both started laughing and spent the rest of the day hitting it.

My head was splitting open by time I got home, so I went straight to bed. The next day I tracked down some more "rush" and introduced my friends to it.

Hanging out with the older kids led to smoking cigarettes, drinking a little beer, and eventually smoking weed. I stopped huffing rush and spent a lot more time smoking weed. I also got exposed to porn and then sex. Several of us were introduced to sex very early by people that should have known better.

This led to very confusing times for many years after. People began to trade weed, alcohol, speed, cocaine, and other things for sex. None of which our parents knew about, nor did any of us want them to. There comes a point where you're not a victim, but a participant. And we knew that if we told, it would be dealt with.

These early pre-teen times were strange, and it didn't feel right, but by the time we were teenagers, it all just became normal.

I CAN TELL YOU, that out of that group, several eventually died from drug and alcohol abuse. Others did time in the joint for rape, theft, and loads of other crimes. And a few even died from HIV.

My early introduction to sex, together with the clouding influence of drugs and booze, confused the reality of what a relationship between two people should look like. Love just became a way to get into your pants, and there needed to be some type of payment to get it.

As a result, I had a stack of girlfriends when I was in junior high and high school. All of those relationships were based on using one another to satisfy a temporary need.

I understand now that the opposite of love is not hate, it is use; when you use someone, you're not loving them, you're just empty and selfish.

CHAPTER 5
CLUB LIFE

When I was about thirteen, I developed a fascination with organizing people. I had seen the show, "The Warriors", and was instantly hooked on colors and cliques. I was never interested in being like the leads in the movie, I was interested in the control.

The very first guy that spoke in the film said, "Can you count, suckers?" He went on to tell you how to control a city by controlling one block at a time, even from the cops. Yep, that interested me being in power, having control. Some people get hooked on dope, some on booze, I was hooked on power.

The small attempts I tried in school never really came together, but once I was riding a street bike at nineteen, things started to change. I got hooked up with a small time crew running guns and dope from one end of the country to the other.

Bear in mind, Wyoming has I-80 and I-25 as well as I-90. If you're running anything from the west to the east, it more than likely comes through here or changes direction here. Sometimes things need to sit still for a while 'till next transport arrives.

That was the hook and my connection to Motorcycle Club life and I loved it. Always one step ahead of the cops and in-step with the most fearsome group of guys you have ever seen.

I found a place I felt I belonged.

I spent a great deal of time reading on knights and secret-societies. I wanted to pull together the thought process that knit men together and built loyalty. So, I would join small groups like motorcycle rights organization and shoot straight to the top. This was because I spoke well and knew how to research well. I was always filled with self-confidence and you couldn't change my mind for nothing.

But the problem was, once I had risen to the top of these little groups, I would start recruiting people that had more of a gang mentality; this would inevitably cause the group to fall apart, or I would end up leaving because the club was too soft.

So I STARTED RUNNING with Clubs like the Bandidos M/C and the SOS. I saw what real outlaw life looked like and I loved it.

ONE NIGHT, we were out at a club called Lovies, where the guys all knew and dated the strippers.

As we rolled up to the doors, Crazy Dave had a big bowie knife on his side, most of us kept ours tucked up in our vest, but he had his on his side.

The bouncer stopped Crazy Dave, "You can't come in here with that." "I can carry a knife. I'm going to carry a knife, I ain't hurting anybody. I'm not causing any trouble," he retorted.

Pretty soon there were several bouncers, our group looked around and thought, "This is no big deal we can beat these guys up." But we wanted to hang out with the strippers and drink beer, so we encouraged Crazy Dave, "Come on Dave, just give up the knife!""FINE!" Dave stabbed the ten inch knife through the little table the bouncer was sitting at, everybody jumped back. "That better be right there when I get back," he yelled.

As we went to go inside, I saw the bouncer try to move the knife, but it was stabbed too far into the table, it wasn't moving. We went in kind of chuckling and start drinking.

Dave was angry and pounding drinks. "Dude, chill out," I said. He looked at me, "Stupid! All that argument over a little bitty knife! They didn't even ask me for my gun!"

He pulled out a 44 magnum with an eight inch barrel from under his colors! "They didn't even ask for this!" As he's waving his gun around, the strippers started screaming. Everybody started running for the door! That's when the police asked us to leave.

AMONG BIKERS AND COWBOYS, it's pretty common to get into scraps, especially at rodeo time. It was rodeo time, we were at the bar and a small fight broke out between us and a bunch of cowboys. The fists were flying and we were just having a good old time!

Fighting was just a natural thing for us. It didn't mean anything. Not everyone has to end up in the hospital; you don't have to beat a guy to death.

The bouncers came in too and started fighting us, so we fought the bouncers! Everyone fought all the way through the bar and into the parking lot. Everyone had something bleeding.

We stood across from each other staring at one another breathing heavy and getting a second wind ready for more. When all of the sudden one of the cowboys reached behind his back. It was obvious he was going for a gun, all of us were looking at him like, "What are you, stupid? We all have guns." If he pulled out a gun, it was all going to go south.

As his hand gripped whatever it was, Scotty, one of the BMC, stepped forward and looked the guy square on, "Better be pulling out a ham and cheese sandwich from back there, because whatever it is, you're gonna eat it."

The guy froze in his tracks, you could see the fear creep over his face, his heart beating a million miles a second.

I busted out laughing,

"What did he just say? A ham and cheese sandwich!"

The rest of the guys including his friends started laughing and the guy just kind of let it go.

I have to tell you that was one of the funniest things I have heard to this day. I have searched for moments to use lines like that and was never quick enough to pull them out.

CHAPTER 6
THE OL' LADY

It was during those years that I met Kristie. We were both working at a local cemetery when we first locked eyes. I gave her a cocky grin and she immediately knew I was going to be trouble... and she liked it.

We quickly became inseparable. Going on motorcycle runs together, camping, traveling, and partying with family and friends. She became, and still is, the love of my life. And so we got hitched in no time at all!

Kristie loved being married to an outlaw with its adventures, the constant drama, and the sense of family that was a part of the lifestyle. And her role as an ol' lady was very important for someone living on the wrong side of the law.

There are a lot of unwritten rules. She knew when not to ask questions and to look the other way. When to wash the blood off of my colors without asking where it came from. And that there may be nights I wouldn't come home and I wasn't going to explain where I had been.

She would follow me anywhere. And she never doubted me. Yet she spent a lot of sleepless nights holding her breath, wondering what the morning would bring. And though she wasn't with God at the time, she sure did a lot of praying for me.

Kristie also had unwritten rules of her own. If I broke them, there would be hell to pay. Case in point, one day when Beef, a friend of mine, was building me a stab proof vest, Kristie made it very clear that if I was joining the BMC, he needed to make the pockets big enough to fit the divorce papers.

I ran with them, but I wasn't going to be a part of them.I knew when to not cross the ol' lady when she stands her ground!

KRISTIE ALSO GAVE me the greatest gift, a daughter, Keshia.

She was all but conceived on the back of a bike. Keshia was raised thinking everyone had beards and were on the rough side. To her, they were family, and it was completely normal to have 15 tattooed uncles hooting and hollering for you at your games.

And she took after her pop's as well. She could tell you the make of a motorcycle, what color the patch was, and what position the rider held just by where they were in the procession of bikes.

Her earliest memory was the feeling of excitement and the smell of leather as we ate some grub on our way to Sturgis. She was convinced that being the daughter of a motorcycle president was similar to that of the daughter of the United States President.

She said, "First off you both have tough guys in black looking out for us and taking orders. Second, whether it's our house or the White House, they were both always full of people!"

And, of all things, she ended up marrying a cowboy! Keshia and Tyler gave us, Trenton, and Paisley. The greatest grandkids ever!

FUNNY AS IT WAS, there is some truth to it. When you walk into anywhere with the club, there is a feeling of power and entitlement. You can see both fear and envy in the faces of the onlookers. In those moments, the feeling of power was ours.

As a family, we were all hooked by the loyalty and brotherhood we experienced in these clubs.

And so when some guys from Casper approached me about starting my own club, it really dug into me. I got it in my head, if I did it, I would form a club that would be different than anything anyone had ever seen. I would build one that had a core value of dedication to family, and to the brotherhood.

I know all clubs think that's what they're doing, but it always ends up with the same bloody mess. Only two ways most clubs end, in prison or in blood.

The need to build loyalty would be my focus and the need to feel elite would be what would bind them together.

CHAPTER 7

THE SOUND OF PIPES ARE CALLING

When I first started thinking about how I would pull a new club off, I was working nights in the oil field as a Steamflood hand, so I had time on my hands. So, first and foremost, I designed a structure from all of the old clubs I had been a part of and made a list of rules to keep us from getting killed. And, last of all, I created a sticker with what would become our insignia.

The three guys that first came to see me about joining were all really nobodies. "Honda", was a skinny little guy that couldn't fight his way out of a wet paper sack, nor would he want to; he was just a pot smoking good time guy.

Then, there was this kid, "Justin", who pushed really hard to join; he had come from a decent family with money, but he was a low-life back-stabbing kind of guy. I won't say a lot about him.

Lastly, "Dude", was about the toughest man of the three and the only one with true outlaw thinking. I eventually found 15 guys, and passed the sticker out to them in the spring of 1994.

I was practicing Asatru, which is a Nordic religion, at the time. So the first meeting happened on the thirteenth moon, per the Nordic belief. We knew that it was time based on casting the rune stones, which we called bones. Rune stones work by pouring them out of a cup, but you have to pour them out onto a specific skin. I had a goat hide and Honda brought over his bones. The bones called the date of and time of the meeting, which was at the rise of the new moon.

The name of the club also came from the bones. Each toss gave just one upturned stone. The first produced the stone of power. The second toss showed the stone of brotherhood. The third stone told of the OutDweller. It was set, the stones had spoken. Oden had called us to live outside of the common people. No longer to be citizens of the norm, but to live outside of them, to feed on them.

THE CLUB MEETING started that night, all fifteen men arrived and filed into my shop. Justin started arguing about the rules right off the get-go, joined by a few others. Justin had brought in people that he thought would help him rule over the club, to gain strength and power. But I had brought in the toughest and unafraid.

When the dust cleared and the fight ended, eight men walked out of that shop and rode off to become nothing. Seven of us swore allegiance to one another in the light of the moon.

Three commitments were uttered in the darkness, the three that would be uttered day after day for the next ten years.

First:

"My honor is loyalty," deep voices repeated after me.

Second:

"I am my brother's keeper," echoed off the walls of the shop.

Third:

"In serving each other, we become free," the final call to arms, and to the brotherhood.

It was some time before patches could be constructed. In the meantime, I made arrangements with 1% clubs (whose leaders I knew) to clear us for starting. They figured we would be just another flash in the pan and die out in a year. But this helped incorporate our entire society within a larger society of tight knit brothers. For me, this was more than just a bike club, this was about changing our community, and becoming more.

We then started gathering prospects and building our funds. No drugs was the rule, at least no powders. We would work for our money at jobs. Yeah, we all worked and I became the safety supervisor. I know, right?! I was good at communicating, rougher than hell, and didn't mind putting people in their place. For the oil field, I was the best kind of safety guy. The kind that might kick your head in if you didn't do it his way.

At that time, I was lifting weights like crazy so I was a 260 pound monster who loved getting bloody. I was drug free and so were most of the club. Meth creeped in a couple of times, but people were lined out and things were corrected. The only drugs that were allowed in the club were things like weed and shrooms.

We even had a small group called, B.O.O.B.S.. It stood for the Benevolent Order Of Bong Smokers. I never joined their ranks. But they had regular meetings and dues for their own little group. Being the president, I knew never to call them after one of their meetings, unless Kristie had cooked a lot of food!

THE CLUB WAS WELL SET the first few years and the roar of all those Harleys sounded awesome! Power would come through the roar of those pipes. They were forever calling us to the road.

My house became the club house and all the brothers were there at least once a week, if not every single day. Our home was never empty and my kid thought it was normal to have twenty to thirty uncles all the time.

All brothers and their families ate at our house. Ol' ladies cooked and split-tails came and went. A split-tail was usually a stripper or girl that is easily passed around, fair game to anyone who didn't have a girl. Sometimes they would stick around for a month or two; other times, they would just stay one night.

But good ol' ladies were well looked after within the organization. Mine was the teacher of all the new ones. Kristie had been around clubs for several years by this time and knew when to speak, shut up, pull a gun, or do whatever it took to keep the brotherhood's secrets. You can have a wife and she may be dang good for you, split-tails come and go, but a solid ol' lady is worth everything, and I had the best!

Kristie would tell brothers all the time if a girlfriend was going to make it or not. She called it one-hundred-percent of the time. Our women weren't patch holders, but they did have an influence. I assure you this, if she had your attention in the bedroom, she had your attention in the world. But if she had the attention of your heart, then she had your attention in the club.

A woman could be a powerful influence. So, I spent time getting to know everyone's ol' lady. I worked very hard at winning their hearts and advising them on their husbands. I would counsel them with their kids, and Kristie filled in where I couldn't or didn't know how.

All the glory of being the boss came to me, but Kristie Eldredge, who didn't have ink or a cut, was in charge as much as I was!

CHAPTER 8
THE SEER

Officers in the club were just like anywhere else. Chapter President, Vice President, Sergeant at Arms, and Secretary/Treasurer. These men were elected every two-years. Most already lived the roles they were elected to. Presidents lead, VP's guided the boss's rules, SA's enforced rules, and the other counted the money and collected the fines.

The club was broken down into several parts. First, were the Knights of Vengeance. These were the brothers that shed blood for the club. If there were things that needed to be tended to, these guys took care of it. They wore a KOV on the bottom of their cut.

The second was the Dark Horse Knights or the DHK. These men were about keeping the club growing and recruiting. They had a focus of taking new lands for the club and recruiting the right kind of members. They were all very well spoken and loyal to a fault. They were in general all family men and could not afford blood on their colors.

The third and final was the KGC, The Knights of the Golden Circle. Their job was purely public relations. They made us look good, and were nice to people. The kind of brothers that were picked out for this was the kind of guy you would want to live next door or teach your kids at school. These guys always knew the radio Dj's and TV anchors and were on good terms with the cops.

Then there were brothers that were just brothers. Getting into any of these groups was invitation only. One of our brothers, Wolfeman, had moved to Salt Lake City and so we talked with the local clubs so he could ride there.

It was no big deal until Wolfeman showed up with Wrench and Derrick who wanted to join the Outdwellers!

"Ok... Let's do this and see what happens."

We patched them out and started a Utah branch.

THE CLUB really started growing and life was intense all the time. We started getting attention from everyone.

Big 1% outfits were meeting with us on a regular basis and demanding we come in under their banner. But we didn't want to be a support club, we wanted to do our own thing!

With all of this attention, I knew we needed direction. So, we went to a witch and had her do a reading on the club to give us a clear path.

Employing a witch was common for me. I had been using this one since the club started to help me build ceremonies.

She read cards for start and invited a male witch to dig deep for guidance. The man was blind, but he was a seer. In our Nordic beliefs that was very powerful.

In this case, as she read the cards, she spoke, "You are able to war against oppression and win."

That's all I needed, but she wasn't done.

"There will be betrayal and you will live leaderless for a time. There is a pain of brothers coming to the surface to destroy all of your hearts."

Then the Seer spoke up. He looked around the room as if he could look into each one of us. He started with Honda Norman and Dude:

"You will waver in your hearts."

"Go pound sand, I'm blood till the end!" Dude retorted.

Honda was scared, and I knew his heart was already failing.

There were nine of us in the room, all full patch holders. The Seer told each of them something of the coming war for our souls, who would run and who would stay.

When he looked at me, he paused long and hard. His eyes seemed to roll up in his head and his voice was raspy which was not normal for him. I leaned forward wanting the blessing of my god, Oden.

"You will receive more power than you have ever known. You will have to pay a price for all you love. You will lose all you have gained, and those that hold you dear..." he paused straining for words, "will hold you in fear."

His blind eyes looked right at me, and touched me with a feather on the back of my head and said, *"You will be lost to this realm."*

I didn't know what any of this meant yet, nor would I for some time. They were predicting the full rise of our club, the change of my belief system, then the complete crash of our MC and the brotherhood!

That night, there were many talks to each of the brothers about the pain in their hearts, and the lost soul of their lives. We all walked away that night and it has never been discussed till I just put it on paper.

CHAPTER 9
THE OUTDWELLERS MC

One thing about belonging to a club is there is always drama. It can be anything from girlfriends trying to kill one of the brothers, to a brother sleeping with a cop's wife. It was always something.

Day to day, life was probably a lot like yours. Get up, go to work, come home to family. Unlike you, we just did it on bikes.

We had two meetings a month, Friday night fights at the bar, and planned runs where we scootered around having a good time.

In order to join the club, you had to prospect after you had hung around for some time. If you were asked to prospect, it was because we saw something in you and invited you in. Prospects had a sponsor, who was in control of their life for nine months on the minimum.

During the prospecting, we would run them through the ringer. Anything a full patch holder asked a prospect they had to do.

Some of those guys would get called at three am to go move furniture or run to the store for a pack of smokes.

Prospects would have to watch over families when brothers were out of town or drop kids off at school.

They were always being pushed. Very few prospects ever truly survived the process. In fact, I would venture to say maybe ten percent made it. There was a reason they were pushed so hard. It wasn't revealed to them until they became a full patch holder.

I would go out of my way every year to buy the most complicated tent to put together. The prospects first job on a run was to get my tent up. The brothers would watch him struggle and get it done sometimes more than one prospect helping. As soon as he was done, the rest of the brothers would point to their tents. In general, by the time the prospect was done with everyone's tent, the mandatory shots and beer chugging, he would be exhausted and drunk.

As he would go to his bike to get his tent, he would find it already set up in a good spot and his bed roll laid out for him on which he would collapse. The lesson here was "I am my brother's keeper."

The brothers would bust your butt all day long, run you day and night, but at the bar, I never saw a prospect buy his own beer or have no one back him during a fight. They learned that loyalty was our core value and violating it, ended violently and permanently.

Most clubs have a patch that reads the initials of the club. A made up example would be DFFD meaning Dogs Forever Forever Dogs. The OutDwellers only had the three links of a chain OOO, OutDweller Only Once. It meant you had one shot to make it into this club and hold onto that patch. The patch was something worth fighting and dying for. Even more importantly, you had to be willing to kill for it, if need be.

Prospects were taught this with constantly being put through the ringer: insulated, threatened, and challenged. To be an OutDweller was to separate yourself from the world and make yourself an independent man that was greater than the walking dead out there.

That's how we saw the world, we saw people as nothing more than mundane idiots given over to a life of being nothing, just simply feeding the machine.

To be an OutDweller set you apart and the pride in the men, ol' ladies and their kids showed it. Other clubs saw it, and the cop noticed too.

A full patch holder had earned all rights in the club. He could vote, hold office, and he stood for everything the club stood for. We were a brotherhood more equal than not.

1% clubs started putting pressure on us to wear a support patch. We were getting pressure from one group that called us to a meeting and leaned on us very heavy.

It was made clear that all 1% clubs were going to have support clubs and it was the only way of survival. Larger 1% clubs had smaller support clubs do all their dirty work. If they needed something illegal done or had a war to fight, the support club was expected to do that.

We said yes to one club, because I was trying to protect us. I will say this was the absolute worst decision I ever made in my life. We sewed their little patch on our vests right over our hearts. And we all started fighting the same day.

Honda and Dude left the club just like the witch had said. It was a painful and angry time for the club. And it lasted for about two-months.

In the meantime, the cops rounded me up and took pictures of my patch. "Do you understand who you are tied up with?"

"Leave me alone," I retorted, "Go pound sand!"

After this, the brothers all came together, "This isn't going to work for us!" "I don't want to be someone's bitch!" They wanted freedom at any cost.

The phone call was made to the president of the Montana chapter of this club. He was less than pleased. In fact, he told me we could not be a club at all, and if we displayed an M/C on our backs we would be shot on sight.

I got off the phone and looked at Kristie, "Looks like we are going to become the OutDwellers boat club".

My phone rang late that night and it was a guy they called Lurch. Lurch was about six foot seven and missing fingers on his left hand. He lost them when a cannon misfired. His claim to fame, was a time he had cut off the head of a snitch and hung it from the back of his bike as he rode through town as a warning to other snitches. He went to jail for a few years. They found he was insane, so his time turned into treatment and he was let back onto the street. Lurch and I were friends.

"Rooster," he said into the phone. That was the name given me by my enemies, "I am going to have to come down there and kill you, my boss said you have to die."

I listened to the struggle in his voice, with the choice he was given. I knew he was telling me he was coming to kill me. It was what he did, even if he didn't want to. I thought for a couple of seconds, "Lurch do you still have that cold? You don't sound so good."

"I am still a little sick, but that doesn't change anything. I am coming to kill you."

My voice clear as it could be, "I understand. I just thought if you were still sick I would drive up to Sheridan so you can kill me there; it will save you two hours of driving."

There was a long pause on the other end of the line. Lurch was tougher than all get out, though not the sharpest man I ever met, but I really did like the guy. Suddenly, I heard laughing as he put together what I had just said.

"I tell you what, Rooster, if you ever show your face in Montana in those colors again, I will shoot you on sight," and the phone went dead.

My wife was staring at me shaking her head, "Are you out of your mind?"

"Naw, you just got to face it as it comes, babe. We need to make some phone calls." I rounded the brothers up and a new era of OutDweller history began.

CHAPTER 10
EVERYTHING CHANGES

F or the most part, everyone thought of us as no threat; but with our short time as a support group, the cops saw us as an outlaw club and we made the FBI list.

For us, this was great news! It meant that clubs across the country would see us as something.

We were a single patch club at the time, a real mom and pop organization, so we stayed underground for a year. That meant that we did not wear patches at all, but we were still growing. In fact, this brought more people wanting to join us than ever before. When we reemerged, it was as a two-patch and no M/C.

We rolled out on a very important day in Wyoming, the Casper Bike Parade, with 300 bikers parading for motorcycle awareness month.

My plan was to let all of them know, including one of the other local clubs, we were still here and had doubled in size.

We didn't join the parade. But knowing the parade route, we would cruise by heading the opposite direction. We wanted to make a statement, we are going the opposite direction of what you are doing, we oppose you and every organization.

Every major turn two-patch holding OutDwellers would ride by going the opposite direction, not waving, just slow, so all had to turn and see the patch. Then, at the last turn, they saw four new prospects making the statement, "we are still here and growing".

Then, as they headed for the home stretch of the parade, we were in a perfect pack, silently saying, we are OutDwellers and we do not stand with you.

I wanted them to know we were not the riding dead, and we didn't need their approval to ride in Wyoming. This single act of complete defiance led to many, many fist fights. If you fought one of us, you fought us all and we always stood our ground, no matter who came against us.

A 1% club out of Colorado sent a member up to Wyoming to check us out. He was trying to get us to come under wing or take some of our members. They had been talking to a member, Lunchbox, behind our backs, and he was now in trouble with the club.

I found out they were coming to his house to get him and talk to him about becoming a member. The entire OutDweller brotherhood met him at his house, "Lunchbox, just what is going on?"

Before he could answer, two of the 1% club's unpatched prospects showed up to retrieve him. I met them in the yard, "He won't be going with you."

Things got a little heated and they left. I turned to the brothers and spread them out a little, "We'll see just how many of these guys are in town in just a second."

I could hear the bikes coming from several blocks away and they were moving fast. I noted that they were only coming from one direction and it was at best two to four bikes. It ended up being three. One full patch holder of the 1% Nation.

He walked into the yard with his chest out and very full of confidence, "When we call, you come!"

We all just stood there saying nothing. He looked around at the circle that had formed around him and he could see guns in every belt. I saw his face as he realized he was in real danger.

"They told me you were a mom and pop club. All I see here is Hitler's youth," his voice was becoming unsure,"If I don't call in, you will have 50 of my brothers up here in the morning!"

I finally spoke up, "Well, they are going to be one short come morning."

As he turned to meet my eyes, I saw true fear creep back into him. He discovered we didn't care and we were *not* afraid.

"Come inside." I said.

He followed me up the stairs and the boys kept his tag-alongs in the yard. Introductions were made and peace between the clubs was laid out.

Our reputation grew as a hard-nose little crew, and meetings with large 1% organizations started becoming part of my monthly life.

I WAS MAINTAINING a job as a safety person and an outlaw. I lived two completely different lives and did quite well in both of them. We had earned the respect of the two major nations who we dealt with all of the time, and so the M/C appeared on our backs once again!

We were gaining notoriety in our little community. And had our fair share of enemies in both Utah and Wyoming. The bigger the club that hated us, the better I liked it. In that life, your enemies make you great.

Fights were a norm for us... and the parties; oh, the parties were famous. We threw huge house parties that people begged to get invited to.

Halloween was our biggest gathering. We would all come in costumes and, man, we would party. We also had the best New Year's Eve party. It would always run till three or four in the morning. More than once, the sun would creep up on us and it would be time to ride your bike home in ten-degree weather; so drunk, your wife had to start the bike, then the crazy chick would get on behind you!

As I SAID, I was powerlifting back then. I was in the gym three days a week, for as many as three to four hours a night. I was well known in the gym and had two guys, Randy and Gordon, that worked out with me all the time. They both rode, but neither were a club brother.

We started one of my club brothers lifting; his name was Conan. He did well for such a little guy. Little meaning tall and skinny, not a 300 pounder like me. Conan got involved with a softball team the gym had. I didn't really think mixing with the general population was a good idea, but he was a grown man.

Randy invited two guys who were brothers to join us lifting. I didn't like either of them. They were both strong, but they were jerks and thought very highly of themselves. I tried to get to know them, but didn't really care for them.

One night, a bunch of the club brothers went down to watch Conan play softball. After the game, we were all rolling out on our bikes and I told Conan, "Let's roll." He decided to hang with the team and drink beer. He was a full patch holder, so he could make his own call. I remember telling him that it was not a good idea, but he felt it was no big deal. So, we left and he headed into their little party.

About two hours later, a fight broke out between the two brothers from the gym and Conan. Then the entire team jumped Conan. The whole thing had been a set up and he didn't see it coming.

They started by picking at our patch, and, when he bowed up, it was their chance to say they were just defending themselves. Conan didn't call any of us after it was over. He knew several of us were headed to the Highland Games in upstate Wyoming, where I and a few of the other boys were competing.

When I returned home, Conan met us in the yard of my house. His head was hung low and he told me what had happened. I ripped his butt for not leaving when I had asked him to. He pulled me aside, "I have to tell you what they said about the patch."

When he was done, I was beyond furious. I wanted them dead.

I know at this point everyone wants to know what was said, but I do not care to repeat it. It was all personal attacks against me and my wife. They made fun of our name and our patch, which deserved a punch in the face.

The fact that the guys who were my friends, like the gym owner who allowed all of this, was beyond me. Yes, Conan should have left, but I also knew in my heart I had allowed him to stay.

The brothers that were at the house blew up. They wanted to take apart the team and their families. I was focused on those two boys.

These "little boys" as the newspaper would later call them were both six foot plus and both benched over 300 pounds and squatted 400 plus pounds. Little was something this eighteen year old and twenty year old were not. The one thing about storytelling in the paper, it's just like a courtroom: you pick a bad guy and turn the world on them.

This was a Sunday evening and the plan was to go down and isolate them on Monday. I would deal with the issue. That night the brothers called one another. They were not going to let me get jumped the way they did Conan, so they planned to meet me at the house after work.

I went to work and brewed all day, getting very angry.

In my mind, the reputation of my club was on the line. I was at war in Utah with two other clubs, they wanted to kill the president of that chapter. I got up from my desk at four, walked into my boss's office and sat down.

"What's going on, Bert?"

He knew I was having a bad day. So, I told him.

"Think heavy on this, Bert. Don't run at it with raw emotions," he advised me.

I stood up from my chair, "I gotta do, what I gotta do."

I knew I was wrong for this hate. Everything in my gut was screaming for me to stop.

I put on my cut, its weight felt like a thousand pounds that day. I fired my bike and road to the house. As I blew down the road, the wind didn't calm me, because my gut-feeling was clouded by anger.

Things for everyone were about to change. I just didn't realize how much.

CHAPTER II
THE FIGHT

One by one, the kickstands hit the asphalt, and engines fell silent. Six pairs of boots stood side by side looking towards the gym doors.

I headed into the building with the Sergeant-at-Arms on my heels. The others guarded both entrances just in case things went south. I cornered the owner of the gym, "What's the deal? Why did you let this happen?"

"Things got out of hand. Just don't do anything at my gym, okay?"

"Did you hear what they said?"

He nodded, "Conan started swinging and everyone didn't really jump him. It was just to calm him down. It was at that point the two brothers took free shots at him."

"This is going to be handled by me or you. Either way, it's going to be handled."

I could tell he understood what I meant, he just didn't want any violence at his gym.

As we exited the door, the first kid's truck drove into the parking lot. We all stood and waited for him to get out and formed a half circle. As he stepped out and put his gym bag in the back of his truck, he threw out his chest.

"What's your problem?" I asked.

"I don't wanna fight," he responded.

At this point, Conan came flying at him with chests bumping, "You don't wanna fight me without all your friends?!"

The two of them started swinging. The rest of us backed away forming a full circle around them. A quick scan of the parking lot revealed one guy in a car and no one else. They had each other in some strange wrestling hold they both apparently knew.

Crack!

Everything froze, they were both breathing hard.

"Have you had enough?" I asked.

"Yes," Conan said. It was at this point I knew he was badly hurt.

"Let him go." They both released each other. Conan started for his bike obviously wounded. Later I would learn he broke his collarbone.

The kid's eyes and mine connected...

"Do you think you've had enough?" I asked him as a smirk came over his face.

The anger hit me, and I looked over at Chaos and thickly said his name.

Our brother Chaos lit the kid up like the fourth of July with about twenty blows to the face before he could even lift his hands. The kid came clean off of his feet and hit the ground hard on his back.

Chaos was on top of him delivering a beating like I'm sure he never had. I called him off.

"You think we are a bunch of punks from what I hear. Sounds to me like you need to fight each one of us to find out who the punk is."

The kid looked up from the ground bleeding from every hole on his head and his eyes swelling "What do I have to do to make this stop?"

I looked down at him wanting to put my boot through his skull, but restrained myself, "Say you're sorry like the little punk you are and kiss my boot."

He did.

We all turned and walked to our bikes. Not a word was spoken as we all went separate directions.

I was rounding the corner when I saw the gym empty out and everyone come running to help their friend. I clearly noticed that they all waited until we left to help him.

The cops were called and the mess began.

I WAS SITTING at my work desk a week later when an informant, who was working in the Casper Police Department, called me. "They're coming for five of you and they're scared, so don't be stupid," the phone hung up.

When the phone rang again it was my Sergeant-at-Arms, "We've got five cops out the front door and I can see a sniper across the street. We going out in a blaze of glory or what?"

I laughed, "Not for a simple assault and battery charge. Stand down and I will see you in jail."

One by one our phones rang, and brother after brother was arrested.

Four of them were in custody, but they only had one more warrant to serve. There was one brother who was there that would not be charged because they couldn't identify him.

A call came from the girl at the front work desk, and she was scared. I was, "needed up front". I looked out my window and could see the police officer, and he was not alone.

I went to my boss's office and told him, "Going to jail, I will be back tomorrow." He thought I was going to get someone out.

As I entered the lobby, I could see the officer's gun was unsnapped.

"I'm clean. You don't need to stir anything in here, man," I reached up and took off my necklace that held my wedding ring and handed it to the girl. I emptied my pockets on her desk, "I'll see you in the morning."

The officer put my hands in cuffs, "You know the drill, Bert." He patted me down and off to jail we went.

. . .

WE WERE ARRESTED around nine in the morning and arraigned at two o'clock in the afternoon. They had five holding cells with five brothers filling them. All the boys were already there when I came walking in.

They started catcalling and whistling. It's jail, folks, not hell. We were cutting up thinking they really didn't have much on us.

They took us one at a time to fingerprint. As Conan started across my cell, I slammed against the door screaming, "I am gonna rape you later, sweetheart! Guard, drop her off in here!"

Conan turned to the guard, "Do you have private cells? If so, I would like to have one, please."

All the guards started laughing and the jokes started us harassing each other.

They dressed us all in orange just to make us look like bad guys I guess. We were all charged with two counts of assault and battery along with lying to the police. We all plead not guilty and got lawyers.

Oh, the newspaper had a heyday saying we had beat a young innocent eighteen year old child and he was hospitalized.

Reality is, he went and got checked at the hospital and received aspirin. Total bill $182. I know, because I had to pay the stupid bill!

CHAPTER 12
LOCK DOWN

So, here were the sentences:

1. Chaos got one year because he was a felon. He turned on the club two-months into his sentence and offered evidence to get out. He never received his patch back and hides from me to this day when he sees me. It's shame, not fear, that causes him to hide. He never had any evidence to give. Any other charges they tried to bring using info he had, fell apart.

2. Sergeant-at-Arms received forty-five days for being present. He has a name and I just use his office out of respect for him. He is only known by his road name to everyone.

3. Prospect turned rat and made stuff up to support their case. He was married to a cop, by the way. He ended up divorced not too long after that and she lost her job. It didn't do either of them any good to be rats. His life as a biker was done and her life as a trusted cop was over. It was exposed that she had been sleeping with the enemy and the cops hate that.

4. Conan got fifteen days for the fight. Funny, he started the whole dang thing and got the least amount of time.

Let me tell ya, the kid himself was stand up, and still is in my eyes. He tried to tell the judge what really went down, but the judge didn't care, and spit out, "You all deserve death sentences for being alive in my town!"

That's how much we were loved by our enemy, the local government. We were now famous to the other clubs because we stood our ground.

5. Then, there was good-ol' me, Bert. I received an offer to do everyone's time if I would confess and call these expensive trials to an end.

"We'll give you thirty days, let everyone else go home and drop their charges." I requested a statue of me in the local park and they hung up the phone. No sense of humor!

I was sentenced to 180 days and the judge was not going to move an inch. "If I could give you life behind bars, you would never see the light of day again" he frothed. I responded, "It was only a fist fight, you know. No stabbing, no shooting; kid took two aspirins and went home."

You gotta love justice.

When I was sentenced, I took off my tie, turned and kissed my wife and my fifteen year old daughter. I looked at a court room full of cops and my club brothers and said, "You know what you have to do. Do it."

The cops thought this meant that the boys were going to harm the jury and judge. But, it actually just meant to keep their heads and keep that patch flying no matter what.

I knew both of the guards. One of them was the brother-in-law to Fat Dog, who I ran with for years. The other was married to a gal who was the Girl-Scout leader for my daughter when she was younger. I live in Wyoming, remember? We all get to know each other in a small town of 60,000.

They sat me down in an office and asked if I was ok. We visited for a few minutes, then they escorted me to the elevator. There was a short guy and a woman with the guards in the elevator. The doors closed and down we went to the van that would take me to jail for the next six-months.

As we entered the van, they set me by the short guy who looked at me, "They give you some time?"

I nodded. The van pulled out to the front of the courthouse and I could see my family as well as the entire club out front. Most of the guys were on phones and the girls were crying. The press was everywhere.

The little guy asked, "Are those your people?"

I nodded.

"It is good to have people", he said.

It was a long ride to the jail even though it wasn't that far. We had cop cars in front and behind us. Like the guys were going to break me out and get me 20 years instead of six months.

Sometimes cops like theatrics.

They unloaded us and took me to be processed in. I knew the guard checking me in; he used to work with me in the oil field.

They gave me my TB shot and took me to the library. I got my bed, pillow, and other items you need for your stay. The guard said, "Pick a book. You're going to be locked down for three days."

I was numb.

I did not pick a book. We climbed the stairs of "F" POD and the door of cell 13 opened. I stepped inside and the door shut behind me. There was a small tweaker standing with his back to me. He had stuff spread all over the top bunk and his bed roll on the bottom bunk.

Without turning around he said, "You can sleep on the floor."

I dropped my stuff and stepped to the middle of the cell; it was very small, a twelve by twelve, "I don't think so", I said.

He faced me and I busted him straight in the mouth. He went flying backwards into the bunks. I mounted him and drew back. He started begging me to stop before his beating even began. I threw all of his stuff on the floor. "Get your butt in your bunk", I said.

He crawled into his bunk and was realizing he was way outmatched. I made my bunk. "If you get out of that bed without my permission, I will beat you plum to death and rape your dead body", I said with a snarl.

I crawled on my bunk and went into a fitful sleep.

The lights never shut off in jail and they buzz endlessly. Around three in the morning, I was awakened by the bed shaking. I looked around and finally asked, "What the hell are you doing?"

"I have to pee. Can I please pee?" he whispered.

I let him out of his bunk and right back to bed.

They served me breakfast in the morning and I gave it to my tweaker, Celly. I started asking him questions about being locked down. He gave me the rundown on the guards and meal times as well as what each POD was for.

He told me, "Try to get into any POD other than "E- POD". It's called 'Thunder Dome'. If you do get in there and they get you in cell one, they will beat you. It is the only cell that there are no cameras on it."

We got out to take a shower and make a phone call. I called my dad first. "I'm sorry for shaming your good name." My dad wept, reassuring me, "it was ok".

I then called my wife and she just cried. The guard told us to get back to our cell, so I told her I loved her and let her go.

As I headed up the stairs, a guy kicked a book out of his cell. I picked it up and read the cover, "The Discipleship of Timothy". I took it into my cell; I could tell it was going to be a long three days.

I HAD no idea what the title meant, but it was something to read and occupy my mind. The book was about 260 pages long, and the first 80 pages or so were missing. As I lay on my bunk reading, the tweaker talked and talked and talked. He gave me a piece of paper for a book marker.

It was a torn out page of something, it read, "The world behind me, the cross before me; no turning back, no turning back."

I had no idea what it was, but I used it. I read it several times as I would read along in my book.

I didn't know who this Timothy guy was, but he was faithful to his people. He was a servant and I understood that. In serving each other, we become free. I understood what brotherhood was for sure.

The world behind me, the cross before me; no turning back, no turning back.

That kept sticking in my head. What does that mean? Was this a poem? Was it a song? I asked the tweaker and he didn't know.

THE DAY CAME that the cell door opened and the three guards were standing there with the nurse. "Let me see your arm," she said. "He's good."

The guards told me to sign a piece of paper stating I understood the rules of the jail. I scratched my name on it. He asked, "Do you need to read it?"

I laughed, "You can't be an Outlaw, if you don't break the law."

He laughed, "Okay, Eldredge, let's go."

"Where are you putting me?"

"E-POD."

I turned to the tweaker who was shaking his head, "Good luck, Outlaw."

We entered E-POD at 8am through the top door of the POD. The guard said, "Cell one." Wait, I thought, cell one is the fighting cell the tweaker told me about? "Great, the lion's den it is", I said with the toughest tone I could muster!

I prepared myself to beat whoever was in that house the second the cops left and make a name for myself. As we entered the doorway, an older guy about 50 was in the house. His eyes grew big as I filled the doorway. I had hate in my face preparing to beat someone down.

The old man sprung up, "I will give you the bottom bunk."

"Chill out," I told him turning to the guard, "You done, honey, or are you waiting for a tip?"

He went on his way. After I set my stuff in the room, I laid down the rule to my new celly, "I am not in the mood for you or anyone else's BS. If you wanna have a go, let's get it done."

He stayed on his bunk, eyes in the book he was reading.

In "E" I saw a guy I knew on the street and approached him. John welcomed me and told me he was doing a year for a gun charge. He gave me a quick rundown of the segregation of the POD. White table here, guys choosing second table, the Mexican table, then the guys just doing time.

"How do I get a seat at the white table?" I asked.

"Dude, you're Bert Eldredge! You're already at this table."

My reputation preceded me on the inside and I knew how to efficiently play politics, so moving to a solid group worked out for me. By the time we locked down that night, all was well and I was established.

WITHIN THE WEEK, I RECEIVED a letter from my wife at mail call. I read it and received two pictures, one of her, and one of my kid. I put them both on the wall and laid back on my bunk. I was reading my Timothy book again when my celly spoke up. "Man, that girl is real cute. She looks like a pirate with those earrings."

"Shut up, and go to sleep," I told him. He must have thought I was kidding because he said it a second time. I came off my bunk, "I told you to shut your mouth about my 15 year old daughter."

He smiled and got out of his bunk, "Well, then she is just the right age, and I am out of here tomorrow." You can imagine the rest... I made him clean up his own blood off the floor after it was done.

He then pushed the button to ask for help. The guards came in and asked what had happened. He told them he fell off his bunk when he was sleeping and hurt himself.

They removed him. I slept that night with no celly.

I eventually ended up with a guy named Weasel in my cell. He was a good dude, just a tweaker that had been down a few times. He showed me a million tricks about running a store and collecting on debts. As well as how to make a bunk, so you could sleep on it and not have a stiff back. He and I did really well together. He also knew how to shut his mouth. And, so, I fell into a routine fairly fast.

CHAPTER 13
NO MORE SCREAM

About a month later, after the 6 pm count, there were a bunch of us out in the POD watching TV. Mind you all day, every day is "busy" in the jail. You got guys working out, sleeping, playing cards, dominos, and chess. The most violent game of all is Monopoly. I've seen a lot of people get a beating over that game.

Each POD was broken into two tiers, upper and lower. On either side of the POD there were stairs leading to the top tier. The top tier had bars all along the railing, so no one could be thrown off or jump. Each of the cells were numbered. During lock down time, you went into your "house" with your cell-mate, they locked you down for count, then you were allowed out. During this time, you were never allowed to be in anyone else's house. Being caught doing so, may result in a week or month in "F" POD. Or, at a minimum, you may get locked down in your own cell for 24 hours.

The showers were all down stairs in the open, so the guards could see you showering. It was a pain with 47 inmates in there, so you always needed to plan showering out. Some of them, dang sure could have used a shower a little more often. But that's another story.

As we sat there watching TV, we heard a loud bang. Someone from the other POD had slid a note through the door and kicked it. This was commonly known as a mail call. My buddy, Whitey headed up the stairs at a jog and I was right behind him.

As he got to the top of the stairs and went to snag the note, I turned and looked at the tower. I could see the officer looking at us, "Don't grab it!"

"Too late..." was the reply.

I could see the guard calling on his radio and turning to leave the tower. "Brother, you'd better eat that note" was my advice, as we headed down the top tier.

I knew we were hit and this could bring a new charge.

As we moved down the tier, I looked into E-20, which was the house right in the middle of the POD. There were about twelve guys seated on the floor in there and I could hear the POD door opening. The guards were coming.

Lock down is better than a new charge, I thought to myself, so I stepped through the door.

The two leaders sat up straight on the bunk and all eyes were fixed on me. One of the leaders was the little guy that rode with me the day I was sentenced. The other was one I didn't even notice in the POD before. Dale Hunt was the small guy, and the other was Jeremy Poole. It was obvious to me that they were in charge here.

"What's going on here?", I asked.

The guards went flying behind me and grabbed up Whitey as Jeremey said, "Bible study."

Dale asked, "Are you down with Jesus?"

AS I TURNED TO GO, time stopped. Everything went dead silent. No people making noise, the cops grabbing up a fighting Whitey were silent. I could see it all, I just couldn't hear anything, and everything was moving real slow.

BOOM

A thundering crash hit me like I was hanging onto a bass drum at a concert. It was so loud it scared me, and I thought the walls were caving in. My eyes were fixed on the scene below me, each inmate doing inmate things, the brightness of their orange outfits. A loud voice seemed to come from inside of me, *"This is how you're going to spend the rest of your life."*

I answered out loud, "Not me, man. I am way smarter than these idiots. I'm smarter than the pigs any day."

BOOM

The whole scene in front of me changed. I could see my wife and my kid. My daughter, her eyes wide watching me punch holes in the wall and yell at her mother. I could see that she was starting to see this as normal. I could see my wife lying in bed at night waiting for me to come home from strip clubs and meetings, where some of the men didn't go home.

I could see her fear of one day me not returning to her. I could see the broken heart in her from the times I pushed our marriage to degrees it should never have been pushed.

I could see my face in her eyes filled with burning rage, that she was just trying to survive and not end up like other women in her family had.

I could smell the blood on her hands as she helped me get it off my colors and my cut. I could see her loyalty even though she didn't even understand why some days. I could see that living with men wanting her husband dead was becoming normal to her.

I opened my mouth to say, "NO! This isn't right! I am a family guy, they understand!" But nothing came out, my voice seemed to not work, my feet weighed a million pounds and my hands felt tied to my side.

BOOM

The loud sound of bike pipes roaring in my ears. Laughing, screaming and crying were all one giant mess in my head. I could hear brothers cussing and stomping someone down. I could see scene after scene of families being torn apart. The women once having men they loved turning to men they no longer even knew.

Men that were strong and brave being reduced to fearful; the fear of not fitting in, or losing their patch, or having their cut torn from their back and beat. So afraid that they did what they knew in their hearts was wrong, until the wrong became normal and seemed sane.

I saw each one of their hearts.

Hearts that had bound themselves to mine in oaths made to a god called the OutDwellers M/C. In their oaths, they bound all the hate each of them had to unite under one goal for self-glorification.

I saw bikes rip down the highway with gates standing wide in front of them. Each going to his death filled with the burning fire of hatred in his heart, convinced it was love of brotherhood.

That fire inside of me burned not only my family, but also my brothers' whom I claimed to love.

I, for the first time, was filled with fear. My whole body shook. My mouth dry, my fists clenched, my heart pounding. I had never been afraid before in my life, but I could feel what terror truly felt like in this moment.

BOOM

Everything went pitch black. Silence filled the air. A silence so deafening it hurt. A single scream arose from the darkness. It was a sound familiar to me. It was a scream that had woken me up for years. I squinted my eyes to see.

Nothing.

My eyes suddenly began to see in the dark as faint illumination seemed to come from small cracks in the wall.

I looked around.

The scream again filled the air only louder this time and it horrified me. I could see the walls were like a cave, all stone and rough hewed. It wasn't a cave, it was a TOMB!

Where is this? Why am I in a tomb? My eyes were starting to adjust to the darkness. The small cracks in the stone seem to let in just enough light to see. I started to understand what I was seeing.

The scream again filled the air. Where was that coming from? I suddenly started to see things I did not want to see.

I saw every single act of violence I had ever done.

I saw the damaged lives of victim after victim.

I heard girls crying and men trying to figure out why.

Broken marriages, broken lives. So many hurts, so many damaged people and it was ME! All me, in each and every case, doing the damage and inflecting each and every wound in those people.

Suddenly, in a flash they were no more and it was quiet. There was just one left and he was curled up in the corner. He was afraid and he was weeping. I started towards him and he screamed. He was that scream! It was him! My first victim, the little boy who never cried, but was lost and alone. I beat him down, I made him mind, I told him to quit being a wuss and stand the hell up; I hurt this kid and never let him out of the darkness.

I finally spoke.

"Please," a long pause, "Please, let me see you."

My eyes filled with tears and my shoulders sank. I felt sick to my stomach. He stood with his face still covered. His hands dropped, tears flooding down his face...

It was me.

It was the eight year old me standing in the middle of my stone heart crying for a brother, a brother I never allowed myself to weep for. He was the target of my hatred. He had feelings, he cared, he was clueless, he was weak. He was my first victim.

For the first time in my life, I didn't want to be me.

A VERY LARGE crack had appeared in my wall. I couldn't figure out how I got here. I was in my heart, the tomb of my making. I looked through the crack and I saw Him. He was stripped naked; He was bloody from one end to the other. He wore a crown of thorns. He was struggling to stand, yet had strength like a lion. I realized the thunder was the cross on His shoulder, beating against my heart.

"If you let me in, I will be your Savior. if you let me in, I will be your King."

I turned and looked in my heart. Who could forgive all of this? Who would want a piece of trash like me? No way, no how. Could this Jesus forgive any of this?

I looked around, looking for a place to run. I saw a door with a latch. "I can't continue to live like this! I don't want to be here! I can't take this fire in me anymore, this hate!"

My hand shaking, sweat pouring from me, fear gripping every fiber of my being, I reached for the latch. I started to lift it and the door burst open.

As He came through the door, He was no longer beat down. All I can describe Him to you as is a brilliant light. He was perfect in every way. Overwhelming in Glory!

His cross still over His shoulder, He hoisted it high and stabbed it deep in my heart. A flood of light flashed so bright before my eyes, I was blind. I heard from behind me "Are you down with Jesus?"

It was Dale and I was standing in the door of E-20 looking out into the POD. I felt different, I felt changed, and I was free. I turned back around to them and said, "I am down with Jesus." I sat down cross legged on the floor and Dale and Jeremy began to teach on the love of Jesus Christ.

I KNOW from the moment I turned to leave until I turned back around was a second. It felt as though I had been gone for days. I left the cell and went to my cell E-1 and it was time for count. I told my celly, Weasel, "Dude, I am going to pray tonight."

"Whatever floats your boat" was his response.

As the guards finished their duties and the lights went to dim, I went to my knees not knowing how to communicate with the Man that had just taken over my life. Bear in mind, Weasel was not a believer at all, I started out, "Dear God." To which Weasel responded, " Try 'Merciful Father'. You're not writing a letter."

So, I started again, "Merciful Father, thank you for saving me. Thank you for my time here. Thank you for not allowing me to perish in the flames of my hatred. I have done wrong and you know what I have done. I have murdered, I have stolen..."

Weasel kicked me in the side and walked over to the speaker in the wall. He wrapped a bunch of toilet paper around his hand and soaked it in water, then slapped it over the speaker. "Brother, if you're going to confess to God, don't be so dumb to confess to the cops."

I was thankful for him, he was spot on for protecting me. I confessed everything God had shown me that was offensive to Him that night. I prayed 'till four in the morning and was thankful for forgiveness. My head hit my pillow long after Weasel had gone to sleep.

God was real after all. Far from causing or ignoring what happened to my brother, I now understood that God wept with me, because He loved us both. And, so, I slept for the first time since Little-Loyd's death, with no scream to wake me up.

CHAPTER 14
FREEDOM

For the next five months in jail, Dale and Jeremy helped me understand the Bible. I was thirsty like the dusty prairie I grew up in, and studied every day.

Quinten, the jailhouse pastor also prayed with me often and taught me how to be a real Christian. Not the polyester suit wearing Christian, never putting on a front, but how to become what God had created me to be.

He also sent me my first Bible. I still have it to this day. I remember waiting at mail call and they handed me the Bible. It was Blue. Blue? Really, blue? I thought all Bibles were black or brown, but this thing was blue. I guess Jesus wanted me to know my Blue Book value, I am pretty expensive and hold my value pretty dang well!

The night before I was released, it was the 11 pm count. I had a young celly, Anthony. He was a nineteen year old kid who had been bunking with me for six weeks or so. He was really small, so I took him under my wing and protected him. He would claim to be a believer, but he and I knew it was all superficial.

I said, "Come on, Anthony. It is time to pray."

We laid a blanket out on the floor and got down on our faces. I was due to be released at five in the afternoon the next day. I was going into a world I knew, but as a creation nobody else knew.

"Hang tough, Anthony, I have a couple of prayers to go first. After I'm done, we can open up with free praying." Just to explain, I had written a prayer I had heard in a movie that was fitting:

"MERCIFUL FATHER, I have squandered my day with plans for many things and this was not among them. For all the things I did not do, but should have, for all the people I should have loved, but didn't, for all the joy I did not bring, but should have, I pray for Your forgiveness.

Father, Creator of all that is good and all that is light, hear my cry from the darkness. Bless me, indeed that my territory may be great. Bless me, that all will know what you have done in my life. Bless me not because of my worthiness', but because of the faithfulness of Jesus. Let my name be known with His name, let my heart be one with His heart.

As You and He are one, let me and He be one, bind me Holy Spirit in your sacred love with the Holy Trinity that I may be filled with Your light and goodness. In the name of the Risen King Jesus Christ, Amen."

. . .

I WEPT UNASHAMED FOR HOURS, as I prayed for my brothers and their families. My heart was filled with anguish, as I thought of what my wife would feel about me when I returned a different man than had left six-months before.

I begged the Lord that I would not lose what I had found. That God would use me, push me and love me. And, so, we prayed for hours and hours. About 3:30 or 4:00 AM we crawled into our bunks.

Anthony quipped, "One last prayer, Bert... Lord, grant that they would screw up the time and let Bert out early so he doesn't have to wait all day. Amen."

We both laughed, "Anthony, that judge said every minute of every day, and he meant it." I was chuckling, as I went to sleep.

"ELDREDGE, ROLL UP!" came the call over the squawk box. My eyes barely open, I could see it wasn't lights on. It was the tower guard, Troy. "Eldredge, get up! Roll up!"

Now I was angry, I rolled over in my bunk and yelled at him "What are you talking about? It isn't even daylight outside! You taking me to holding or what?"

"The LT wants you up and out of here now. Roll up your gear, and get out of here! I'm not kidding!"

I was now standing in the middle of the room in my underwear packing stuff as fast as I could. Anthony leaped off his bunk and started helping me.

"God is real, Bert!" He said as he started to cry.

"He is real, Anthony, and He loves us," I said as I hugged the little guy.

"He heard my prayer for you and He answered it." Anthony shouted dumbfounded.

I heard the door pop and the POD door open. It was 5 AM. I put on my orange pants and shirt for the last time, and looked at a very scared kid standing alone in the cell. "It's time, Anthony. No more messing around. Repeat after me. Jesus, I am yours, save me." Anthony repeated it.

Resting my hand on his shoulder, I looked him in the eyes, "That's it, little brother. It is that simple. He loves you and you're His now."

Sadly, Anthony died later that year, but having visited him a few times, I know he died as a believer. Man, those words make me homesick for heaven.

WHEN I STEPPED into the parking lot, the air was cool and fresh on my face. My dad's truck pulled up and I got in. He was aglow with joy to see his son.

We drove across town and I was left standing in the street in front of my house. I went to the door and tried it. Locked, as it should be.

I knocked and, in a few seconds, the curtain drew back. Kristie's face was looking at mine through glass just like at the jail. I watched as her eyes tried to send a clear message to her brain that she was looking at her husband.

She started yelling and tore the door almost off its hinges!

"Why? How? When? Why? Who? How?" she exclaimed, as she hugged and kissed my face.

"Calm down," I told her, "They let me out early."

I walked through the house as she got dressed. Brothers on the couch, brothers on the floor, brothers down stairs. I walked room to room waking them up.

I walked out to my shop and the other love my life, my bike, was behind like eight other bikes.

Wolfeman was standing behind me all of the sudden and hugged me, "Welcome home, brother!"

I pointed to his bike and he nodded. I fired up his ride and put my foot on the clutch and hands on the ape hangers. I reached down and put the jockey shift into first gear and rapped her out and blew down the street.

Conan came out of nowhere on his bike and we rode through town at 6 AM just loving the sound of pipes and speeding like wild-men! My colors on my back and knees in the breeze.

My family threw a giant party that afternoon for me. The entire club was there and lots of friends and family, even guys I worked with.

Happily, I took the little calendar I had made and set it on fire. That is time they can never take away from me again. Debt paid in full.

CHAPTER 15

18 MONTHS OF STRUGGLE

With the club now back together, we had a lot of ground to make up. Not much had been done since I was down; it was like the whole world was on pause. I had six-months left on paper to finish up my probation, but there were no club restrictions. So, I started getting the club back in a groove of meeting along with the public-relations repair.

The phone rang about my third day home and it was the world president of a very large 1% nation. He was coming to have dinner with me. The meeting was set and we met at a restaurant. He was different from the guy that was boss before him. He was very business and zero emotion. His question was *asking* us, not telling us to become a part of their nation. He respected that I stood my ground and that I was willing to go to jail for my cut.

Agreements were made to not become a support group, but to work with them in future growth. We had made a giant leap forward in the club world. I could feel in my gut I was

making a deal with the devil and it was not going to end well.

The next thing I knew, one of the brothers got me to a meeting with another large 1% Nation. They had moved their presidents' meeting to Casper to meet with us. Every president, including their world president, rode in to town. I met with men from around the globe all joined in with one focus. It looked like everything I could ever want, but it was wrong and I knew it.

I respected these guys and respected their organization. When the offer was set on the table to patch over I said, "no". I didn't stand up and shout, "No!" It was a lot quieter than the normal me. I rode away that night knowing that my brothers were now confused.

We were at war in Utah trying to build a chapter and these guys could change that. We would grow not just two states, but gain members worldwide overnight. This life I used to love felt filthy to me. My cut weighed a million pounds as I rode into town that night. I could have had a thousand OutDwellers with me and I would have still felt alone.

OVER THE NEXT YEAR, we struggled to keep it together. I would roll out of bed every Sunday morning and look at Kristie, "Do you want to go to church?"

The answer was always a cold, flat, "no'.

I knew she hated this new me. She did not like the edge that I lost.

I would invite my brothers to church and get a lot of no's as well.

I was not having good luck in the local church body anyway. I would show up with a Mohawk, patch, on a bike, and you could see in their faces they wanted me out. I just didn't fit anymore in anything.

My marriage was rough, my brothers would see me flip out, kick the door of a car in, beat a driver down for almost hitting me, and then pray because I was in shambles.

I was trying to walk between two worlds and nobody was walking with me, nobody.

Every day, there was always some new drama, and the club brothers were growing frustrated with me. I didn't blame them. I was trying to become a new guy and they needed the old guy.

I STRETCHED out one night in my living room. One of my club brothers was living down stairs. I started praying.

"God free me from the evil that is always ready inside of me. The old man is still so alive in me and I hate him. Please, I beg you! You promised you would completely free me, so set me free!"

My cut was hanging on a chair in the living room. I raised my eyes from the floor up to it and knew that was still holding onto me. The oaths made, blood spilled, the brotherhood bond was still hanging on to me.

As I went to bed that night I whispered to God, "Free me, I am yours. Save me." I could feel the darkness in the room. My eyes flew open, I knew someone was standing next to the bed. I leapt to my feet in the bed and threw my wife into the closet.

I was facing a shadow, I started swinging and screaming. The shadow looked like a man and I could feel its hate. It was pure rage. Punch after punch did nothing as I battled the shadow.

All of the sudden, I could hear Kristie screaming my name and the light was on. My bed was completely torn apart, the room was destroyed, and my brother was in the doorway with a .45 pointed into the room. I was covered in sweat.

"Dude, what the hell?" was all he said.

"I must have been dreaming", I lied. As he left, Kris helped me put the room back together. I kept telling her, I was just dreaming, and she said, "If you were dreaming, what were you making contact with as you were swinging?"

I just stared at her and finished putting things back together. I knew God had answered my prayer.

What I was fighting was all of the hate from inside of me. It had manifested as a shadow of my old-self and was fighting back. The darkness always calling me back, and I was not going to turn.

The little piece of paper I had found in jail and used for a book marker finally made sense: "The cross before me, the world behind, no turning back, no turning back."

CHAPTER 16
THE ESKIMO RUN

It was about six-months out from probation, we were about to do a ride that we called, "The Eskimo Run". It was always held in the first weekend in January.

I had just met a preacher by the name of Wes. He had a bike and decided that he and some of the Christian Motorcycle Association (CMA) were going with us. We had become friends with CMA and didn't mind them hanging around.

The run started in the afternoon at a bike shop and was going to bounce around town into several bars ending at the Wonder Bar. My head was focused on just keeping the club together, not where it belonged. I ran none of my security checks and forgot what it meant to be an outlaw for a day, I guess.

At the end of the run we pulled into the Wonder Bar and parked our bikes. We paid no attention to detail. My mind was on getting this run under our belt and moving on.

As we entered the bar, there were roughly 100 guys from another club that we were at war with. I had led us right into a trap.

I knew we were in trouble and none of us had a gun that day. I soon found myself pressed in on all sides, and the president of this other club in front of me. He droned on about all the reasons he hated us. And I told him, "If you had the guts, we would tit for tat and you and I could settle this."

"No, if we fight one, we fight all."

"Then, let's get outside and get it the F@%K on!" I started pressing my way through his people spitting in their faces. I had thirteen men step outside. Thirteen OutDwellers lined up and prepared themselves. My dad, who was in his late sixties, stepped out with us and started arguing with them.

Their State President was standing next to a guy I didn't know and that guy snarled, "We'll be havin' those colors."

I stepped towards him, "Come and get 'em!"

I started swinging.

I was jumped by 10 men and they got me to my hands and knees. They were hitting me in the face and kicking me in the head. I kept trying to get back up, but I was struggling with so much weight on me. But they could not get my cut off of me.

They started hitting me with beer bottles, breaking several over my head. One guy kept trying to stab me in the face with the broken bottle, but I kept his hand trapped. Unfortunately, that didn't allow me the use of my hands, so my wife jumped on the pile and started peeling guys off of me.

When I got down to seven or so, I got to my feet and started swinging again.

You could hear the sirens coming and they took their sweet time. We were two blocks from the police station in Casper and the cops took almost thirty minutes to respond. That to me is what scared cops look like.

When I had gotten to my feet, the other club was starting to run and my brothers were having their way cracking heads. I went to drill a guy as I exited, and a giant arm grabbed me, it was my dad, "Let's go, boy!" He was trying to get me out of there before the cops got me.

Three of us made our way to my dad's truck and got in the back. I was bleeding badly and my dad drove us to the hospital. My other brothers were not as bad off, so they made calls and got guns. Then the doctors separated me from the other club guys that were in the hospital, and there were several of them.

My younger brother, Bobby, had been stabbed in the shoulder and the ear as they cut his colors. He fought them back and still had them in his hand. There were times in that fight I was holding on to my cut with two fingers and putting them back on. We fought a bloody nasty fight for those colors and not one OutDweller lost his patch to the enemy.

We all gathered up at my house and we were on lock down. More guns than most sporting goods stores were in my house, shop and down the street. We were covered from all angles in the event of a drive by.

I started making calls to the big clubs. By the time I hung up with two of them, I realized it was a sanctioned hit. The 1%'rs that "thought so much of us" had used a small club to attack us. More than that they had granted a green light on ending me.

It wasn't too long later that I discovered the local cops knew two-weeks in advance when and where this was going down. They used it to gain funds for a gang task force. Typical life for an outlaw, but don't think I sat around feeling sorry for myself. The problem was now what to do about getting back at them. ALL OF THEM!

MONDAY AFTER WORK I rode home and Pastor Wes was sitting on his bike in my driveway. I slid off my bike,"What are you doing at my house?" I asked.

"Why didn't you come to church yesterday? You said you would come to church", Wes asked.

I looked at him like he was freaking nuts. He had just been a witness to the insanity I saw as normal and he invited me to his church? After watching a gang fight?

"Are you flipping nuts?" I was shaking my head. "Why would you want a monster like me in your church? What you saw yesterday is my life, dude!" I was shocked. Mind you, I used much fouler language.

"I told my congregation everything that happened yesterday. I told them you tried to get out of getting everyone hurt, you tried to get it to end. In the end, when you saw no way out, you fought."

My eyes fell to the ground. I was feeling the weight of what I needed to do. I had to kill at least three people to make this right for my club, that was going to lead to my death and many more killings.

This preacher was out of his mind. I figured God must be about ready to give up on my stupid self... Wes waited and finally said, "Next Sunday then?" I was speechless and nodded my head in confused agreement. He fired up his bike and drove off.

Numb, I turned and walked into the house, into my room to pray and read my blue Bible. Jesus said, "Blessed be the peacemakers for they shall be called the sons of God." I was a man of war. My heart, mind and hands had always been at war. I didn't know how to live in peace. And how was I going to tell my brothers?

"NO RETALIATION! You have got to be kidding me!"

My officers were less than pleased with my decision.

Hollywood screamed, "They put a knife to my throat! They tried to take our colors, man!"

The brothers could not wrap their minds around my choice to not fight back. I was caught between what was normal and what should be normal. I had no idea how to deal with any of this as a Christian, and my brothers really could care less why I was trying to be a nicer guy!

They tried to take our colors, but they didn't.

They tried to kill a few of us, but they didn't.

We were going to have to figure out who was really the enemy. The 1%'rs sanctioned it, the cops sanctioned it. We were a club of about forty-eight guys fighting clubs with thousands of members. This is what we had been doing since the beginning, but now they were aligning themselves with one another.

How much longer could I live between two worlds?

CHAPTER 17
THE SEPERATION

It was six in the morning by the time we rolled away from the Utah Chapters patch ceremony. The air was cool and it smelled of rain. Kristie was on the back of my bike squeezing me tight. I felt her bury her face in my back just like I used to do with my brother Lloyd. And I almost lost my breath like when I was a kid as we caught the highway.

It had been a long two-years since that scrap on the Eskimo run, and the club was growing so fast I was shaking hands with new patch members I didn't even know.

But, in the cool morning air, I could feel it in my gut, what was going to take place in the next few hours was going to change our lives forever.

All patch holders had been called and told to bring their ol' ladies to meet in Wolfeman's garage.

The street was covered with bikes. And I was pacing in the living room, asking God to guide me with the direction this needed to go when Wolfeman stepped in front of me.

"It's over brother," I said.

I will never forget his eyes as he looked up at me, they filled with tears and he said, "I know, but I don't want it to be."

We hugged and slapped each other on the back, I took a deep breath and said, "Let's do it."

I STEPPED into the room and looked around at the brotherhood that was built off a sticker I made up on a night shift.

I could hear the witch's words, as I looked back, I saw they were all true.

Even the demons knew, once Jesus had a hold of me, it was all over for this life.

The meeting and what was said is between me and them.

AT THE END of the meeting, we parted company with dates set to bury our colors, close all chapters, and end the OutDwellers MC.

A lot of hurt and lost people left that garage.

My heart broke because I was watching the destruction of my family. Ten-years we had worked on this and ten-years were now gone. Lots of blood spilled, lots of tears cried. Now it was coming to an end.

Exactly ten-years to the day of the first meeting, the Brothers rolled out on their bikes in Casper, Wyoming. We rented a small bar about forty-five miles out of town. We gave the guy

$1500 and said we are going to drink that, then pay for whatever else we drank.

We had a small bike rodeo with our families, it was something we all loved, and just had a blast. We sent our families home and we began to party like the sun was never going to come up again. For this patch and this crew, it wasn't.

We drank that bar dry and had the time of our outlaw lives. The morning came and we all pulled ourselves together. The OutDwellers rode off into the sunrise never to don colors again.

CHAPTER 18
THE NEW PATCH

The brothers hung around off an, on for about a year afterward. They were broken and looking for a new life. We were on different paths now and they eventually found their way.

I was done with the life and had no intention of joining another club, nor did I want to. That is until God told me in my prayer time one evening that I was going to join the CMA.

I told him NOPE!

But the Lord has a way of convincing you to do what you would never do. I was living proof of that. So, when I finally broke and talked to CMA about it, they, of course, wanted me to join.

"Fools," I thought, "Do you not know what it's like when I have power and a patch?"

The night before I was due to put on the patch, I laid in my front yard and begged God not to make me do this. CMA was everything I did not want to be.

I did not want to be in a club.

I did not want to get a patch on me again.

I thought Christ would want me free of this lifestyle. But, as the sun came up, I clearly heard,

"You know not what you will suffer for my name."

Paul came to my mind. God never took him anywhere He didn't need him or use him. I just had to be willing.

I rose up, went into the house, gathered up my wife and headed down the road. By the way, she was pissed! Yay me, new club, angry wife, what was different?

Kristie never said she was mad, but she had reservations. We had left our family for a bunch of folks she didn't trust, into a faith she didn't have. My wife was still not a believer.

A few of my old brothers were there that day as they initiated me into the CMA. Nomad (My oldest and dearest friend) looked me in the eye and said, "I will follow you anywhere. But not here."

THROUGH THE NEXT ELEVEN MONTHS, things were way different than I was used to. And I met a lot of Christians. Some good, some not so good. I met the CMA state coordinator, and he asked me to go with him to Colorado to a large bike show.

I was about to lay eyes on all of the nations for the first time since I had buried my colors. All 1% nations are at this show. I saw prospects move rather quickly once I was identified.

We crossed by booth after booth of the clubs selling their support stuff and I saw the same thing. Entire groups that used to party with me and want me to spend time with them turned their backs.

They showed me their unity in their disapproval of the patch I was now wearing. They turned their backs on me to show me the ultimate disrespect, putting up a wall.

My heart sank with each booth. I was all out of friends and all out of brothers. The CMA were nice enough, but they weren't a club by any stretch of the imagination.

But I belonged to more than just a club now, I belonged to God's fraternity. And, in my time of feeling the loss of my old friends, He brought me a gift.

My wife had gone on a women's retreat with some of the CMA women. Upon their return, I went out to meet them. The girls all jumped out of the car, hugged Kris, unloaded her bags, jumped back in and sped away.

I was standing on the sidewalk thinking, "What's their issue?" I turned around to look at Kristie and she had this glow to her. I dropped the bags, grabbed her and squeezed her. "You got saved this weekend?!" It was written all over her face! My wife was always a good person and loved people like no other, but it was in this moment I truly saw the beauty she was to the Lord. He loved her so much, and now she loved Him as well.

I was no longer alone in this walk.

CHAPTER 19
THE ROUGHNECK

A few months later, CMA got invited to an event called, "The Round Up Breakfast". It was a pretty big to-do as there were about three thousand men there. They wanted CMA to ride up on our motorcycles, because it's a man thing, you know, and to show up to the event early to pray.

So, I rode up at about 6 AM and saw this guy leaning up against a piece of crap car. He turns to me and says, "You up here to pray?"

"No, I'm just up here to cruise around and see what idiots are leaning on their car."

He laughed.

"Good point, who else would be up here at six in the morning?"

Don Hinton and I became friends immediately because he had a sense of humor and wasn't a big cry baby.

LATER THAT MORNING, as the event was about to begin, Pastor Wes came up and volun-told me, "I want you to pray with people."

"Dude, I don't know enough about any of this to pray with anyone!"

"You'll be fine," and he put a white tag around my neck to be a part of the prayer team.

To my surprise, the man with the crap car was a main speaker. I was wrapt attention as Don gave his moving testimony. But, just as he was finishing, he asked, "If anyone would like to give their hearts to Christ, please, come up to the front to have someone pray with you."

Wait, I was standing in the front. And I had this white tag around my neck!

Through bulging eyes, I could see loads of people coming out of the bleachers to give their lives to Christ. And, so, I did the only thing I could think of, I bowed my head and closed my eyes.

"I don't know how to help any of these people..." I started praying.

Just then, the air next to me was filled with diesel and oil stink. I know what that stink is. All I've ever worked in outside of ranching was the oil field. It's invert (Oil based mud), you get that smell when you're a roughneck.

When I opened my eyes, there was a kid in front of me.

He told me, "I was on my way in from the rig. I was telling the Lord, 'This just ain't worth doing anymore. I don't want to keep doing this.'"

Turns out God told him to turn into the event center, though he didn't know any of this was going on. When they gave the altar call, he gave his life to the Lord instead of going home and killing himself.

Though his tears, he smiled at me and said, "When I looked around, I could only see one person that might know what I'm going through."

It's why I was there that day.

I was the only one.

And, in that moment, I truly began to understand gratitude.

That was one of the first times the Lord used me in this manner, to help another person like that. But it had changed me. It was like the old song said, "I was blind, but now I see".

I saw that I was so trapped in my old life; I had no life. I was like a dead man walking. In order for God to bring me back to life, He had to kill the old club life man in order to make me a brand new man.

I would only stay in CMA for a short time after that. But God had done what He needed to do through them.

For one, it made every single person that ever falsely called themselves my friend separate from me permanently.

But, more importantly, that patch said publicly, "I now belonged to Jesus". And I had no fear in calling Him, my Savior!

CHAPTER 20
FORGIVING ENEMIES

Some time later, during my prayer time, the damage I had caused in my reckless years began to play in my mind like a movie. I saw all the people I had hurt.

Some of them I knew I had wronged. But, some of them, didn't make sense to me, like the first ones on God's list of amends, the gym owner and my lifting partner. I argued with God for some time, "Why should I be the one asking for forgiveness? They were the ones that betrayed me!"

He showed me the hate I had in my heart and the damage it was causing in my walk with Christ. And I knew I had to do this. So, I WENT and saw the gym owner first.

I could see he was afraid.

I looked him in the eye and said, "I want to talk about the fight from a few years ago."

He nodded to show he understood.

"I am sorry for...." I paused, my mouth looking for the words. My heart and head were in a full blown argument.

"I am truly sorry for the feelings I've had towards you and your family. I want you to know I need your forgiveness, not for the fight, but for my hate."

He sat there stunned, "You want to apologize to me?"

I nodded.

His face twisted, totally confused. "I... I accept your apology?!"

I spent a few more moments talking about his failing health and his family. I shook his hand and then asked my old lifting partner into the office.

This was a guy that I spent twenty hours a week with and thought the world of. Yet, he turned his back on me during all of this and it cut me very deep.

Through clenched teeth, I said, "I'm here to ask your forgiveness for the hatred I've had for you. You didn't deserve my hate and I'm a different man now."

He gave me a little speech about how what I had done was wrong, but forgivable. To be honest with you, I wanted to stand up and slap him in the mouth, but God started speaking to me so loud it drowned out his voice. God showed me what was in his heart and that He was dealing with him. At the end, I shook his hand and walked out the door.

Relief and release flooded my soul. I sat in my car for over an hour sobbing like a child. Hard does not begin to describe what it is like to forgive your enemies.

Oʜ, but that was nothing compared to the next one. The next one was going to be tough. Months passed as I debated with my pastor about what God was doing with me.

"You have to get this done before your birthday, Bert," he told me.

And, so, the day before my birthday, I finally made the call. It was to the leader of the bike club that jumped us at the bar.

Hᴇ ᴀɴsᴡᴇʀᴇᴅ the phone and we set a meeting in his front yard. I pulled up the same time he did and we stood face to face in the driveway.

This man and I had tried to kill each other several times. We had harmed each other's family and brothers several times. We had fought a war for over ten years.

I took a deep breath and let it rip, "I want to apologize for my hatred towards you. I have found Christ and I do not hate you anymore. I don't want to swap spit or be best buds, but I just can't live my life with any hate in me towards you."

I waited for the response that could be a punch to the face or a gunshot from a hidden club brother of his. Tears started to well up in the corners of his eyes. Mind you, he never cried, but I could see he heard me. Not just with his ears, but he truly heard me.

"Bert, I am a Christian now. I heard you had changed, but now I can see you really are a different person."

I was stunned. We had a long talk that day and have since become friends that embrace each-other whenever we see one-another. This brought healing for two men that no one understands, except Christ.

Had I not listened to God and retaliated, hatred would have been in my life and his till the end of our breathing, but with obedience, healing took place.

NOW WE GET to the last one. He is a Christian I had known for a while. He was a person that led me down some good roads and some bad roads, in Christ's name.

I got sideways with him and our friendship ended with a lot of political play and angry words. I was a young Christian and still attached to a lot of pain.

I tried to contact him through my pastor and he refused to speak to me. I tried endlessly to speak to him, but he would have nothing to do with me. I finally respected his wishes to leave him alone and just prayed it out. The burden rested on me until one day a friend of mine spoke to him and asked if he would ever forgive me. My friend told me, "He said he didn't care anymore and that he was tired of hearing about it."

When my friend said these words, I knew there would be no reconciling with him.

I learned that day that not every relationship we damage can be fixed.

CHAPTER 21
CALLED HIGHER

Soon, God put a call on me even higher that I had ever dreamed. I had developed an insatiable thirst for God. The Bible studies I had been attending just weren't enough anymore. I had too many questions. I wanted to learn history. I wanted to understand where all these stories took place. I wanted to know the Bible inside and out!

And, so, a friend of mine introduced me to the Christian Life School of Theology. As fate would have it, my buddy from the prayer breakfast, Don Hinton, was in charge of it!

"Bert" he said, "I want you to meet my mother, Ms. Janie", and like a mother hen, she quickly took me under her wing. She and Ms. Dottie quickly saw that I was no joke. I was there to learn. I wanted to know Jesus, not just know about Him. And God used this school to open an entirely new chapter in my life.

The next thing I knew, I had an Asssociate's degree, then a Bachelor's in theology, then a Master's degree in Theology.

Then, the crazy school handed me a second Master's in Divinity, and eventually, a Doctorate in Theology!

I gotta tell you that I was a little freaked out. I went from a thug to a pastor with a big piece of paper on the wall. Only God can do this. Only God can take a guy that can barely read into a guy with a doctorate.

SURE, people are drawn to titles. They tout their education above others all the time. And I've had plenty of titles in my life. From the oil field, the clubs, and, now, from a university. My education comes from the streets and the classroom. And I am thankful for both.

But I have to tell you, I have learned from people in jail, prison, and people eating out of a dumpster, just as much as from my professors. Every person has insights you can learn from. And God will always have something to teach you if you're willing to listen.

I once was talking to a homeless man by the name of Moses. He asked, "You believe in this God of yours a lot, don't you"?

I looked at him and said "I know He is the Way, the Truth, and the Life".

The man asked me a question that still rings in my ears."Can your God do anything"? I answered "He can do everything" I said filled with confidence.

"Then your God and my God are not the same God".

I stood there puzzled at what he had just said. Then looking off in the distance, he said, "Listen, son (I was a lot older than him), the God I pray to cannot lie, nor can He force me to love Him. If your God can do that, then He is not God".

And, so, I stood corrected. Even this homeless man understood something about the God of Heaven. Everyone has value in God's eyes. Even bikers, roughnecks, and police. Even witches, strippers, and PhD's.

Because faith in God doesn't come from degrees or titles. It comes from Jesus Christ when He breaks open the tomb of my hard heart with the power of His cross. It came by God transforming my life through incredible and strange miracles that have shown me I can trust Him.

And, so, I am deeply humbled by my education. But, I also fully recognize, they are not the source of my hope, God is!

CHAPTER 22

ANNOINTING

Some time later, I found myself in a little town called LaBarge, Wyoming. Some friends of mine ran a church there called, the Potter's House. And, as we worshipped together, my friend Don stepped up to the mic.

"I want to share with you today a story of a man that has given himself fully to serving God." He said with a grin.

He spoke of the unselfish acts and courage of this person that literally brought a tear to my eye.

I thought, "Wow! They are going to make someone a pastor today?!"

I listened and started looking around to see who they were talking about. Just then, he spun a chair around to the middle of the room. Many of the pastors stood up and walked to the center of the room. I knew the caliber of these folks, they were the real deal, strong and upright.

"This man is going to go into the darkest areas to bring the light."

This man they spoke of sounded like a good dude. I looked around at the two guys I was sure they were talking about and I leaned to my wife and pointed them out.

Don said, "I would like to have John Berton Eldredge come up here, please."

I smiled at the guy I thought it was going to be. He wasn't moving.

They just called his name.

"Bert," Don said, "Would you, please, come up here?"

"Wait, what?" I asked, "Why?"

They all laughed. My wife said in my ear, "Go up front."

I was still wondering, "Why? I must be praying for this... Wait, did he say my name? I am none of the things he just said."

I STOOD up almost like I was drunk and kind of slowly walked toward the group of pastors.

My heart felt as though it was going to jump out of my chest.

They turned me around and sat me in the chair.

Don knelt before me and took off my shoe and sock. He started praying for me as he anointed my foot, hand, and then my head with oil.

The hands of the other pastors rested on my shoulders, head and back. They all prayed and prophesied over me. It felt as if a spiritual helmet rested on my head.

My shoulders had been strapped with responsibilities before, but this was different. It was not gang colors on a cut being slipped on me, but the Glory of our Lord!

My heart was filled with so much joy. My mind thought of everywhere I had been and all that God had brought me through.

They stood me up and introduced me. I was overwhelmed beyond what I know how to describe. Heaven was beckoning me to rise up and lead men. I had done so before wrongly, but this was going to be different.

THE RIDE HOME for my wife and I was heavy. We talked about what this meant and what we were going to do in ministry.

I looked back at all the people God had put in my path to make this moment possible.

The forgiving heart of the man I helped rob as a kid.

The loving parents that stood by me no matter how crazy I was.

The loving wife who stands by me still.

The daughter who came to know Christ and has become such an inspiration to me.

The two jail house inmates Dale Hunt and Jeremy Poole who taught me so much and were brave enough to run a Bible study no matter what others thought.

Quinten Decker, the preacher who spent his own money to buy me a book that changed my life.

My sister Starla who loved me when no one else did, who saw the good in me only her and my wife could see. She had prayed for God to save me, but was confused when I was arrested. She now saw that I was never arrested, I was rescued!

Dale is now with the Lord, and so is Quinten. I miss them both so much, but I never mourn for them. I just get a little homesick thinking of those that have gone before me.

CHAPTER 23
MINISTRY

Months prior to this conference, we had found out that Quinten's cancer had taken a turn for the worse and they were sending him to hospice. Jeremy Poole and I went to visit him. And I continued to go and see Quinten in hospice every Wednesday.

He asked me one time, "Bert, why do you come here every Wednesday?"

"Well, you came to visit me in jail every Wednesday, so I get to come visit you every Wednesday," I responded.

I was still going to school at this point, so I would come in and tell him everything that I was learning, and he would get so excited.

It was an amazing time of fellowship and study together.

Quintin passed after eleven months in hospice. When Jeremy and I attended his funeral, we were asked to speak.

There were nothing, but old people there, except Jeremy and myself.

When Jeremy got up to speak he said, "This place is pretty empty today." Looking around at the room, it could hold almost 150 people, but the chairs were mostly empty.

He continued, "But truth be told, if we could open the gates of the prison and the jail, this building could not contain all the souls that he has touched. So, Bert and I are here today to represent them."

It became my turn to speak and the Lord gave me some good words. Honestly, I don't remember much of what I said, I was numb with grief. But I can tell you this, at the end of it, while walking out the door, Lieutenant Clark from the jail grabbed a hold of my shoulder. "I need to visit with you for a minute."

I figured I was in trouble with him over something. He really did *not* like me. He viewed me as nothing, but trouble. And, so, he had prevented me from coming into the jail to do ministry for five-years now.

He looked me in the eye and said, "I want you to start coming into the jail. Bring in an application, tomorrow. And I will take care of it." God was so good! In whatever I had said, the Lieutenant could see I had changed. And, in this, God honored His servant, with the continuation of Quentin's work, even in death.

I rushed over and put in that application the very next day. By the following Thursday, I was finally accepted as a Chaplain at the Natrona County Detention Center. The very place I had done my time!

. . .

ON MY FIRST DAY, I met two guys in there that were planning to do a Bible study that night, Randy Raver and Bob Kelly.

"Can I tag along?" I asked.

We waited for the guard to come and get us. The door popped and it was the very guard that had let me out many years before. We spoke briefly as we walked into the sally port and the door shut.

My hands started to sweat. We all made small talk as we headed down the hall to the library. This was the room they took me to get a mattress and a pillow.

They called out the first POD. The door opened and a bunch of guys in orange came strolling in.

We started the study and I gave my testimony. I spoke about being in "E" POD and they all looked at me funny. POD after POD came in and I gave my testimony which drew snickers several times. I think they thought I was kidding.

A group of women came into the room and sat. We all started chatting and finding out where everyone stood with Christ and, all of the sudden, something clicked in me. "What POD are you ladies in?"

I was thinking the women should have come from "B" POD. They all looked at me and said, "'E' POD."

I looked at Randy and Bob and we all started laughing!

No wonder those guys couldn't figure out why I had been locked up in "E" POD! It had been the Female POD for about 5-years at that point. We all had a good laugh.

God has had me in that jail preaching Thursday nights ever since.

GOD EXPANDED my ministry since those days. I now speak at churches to encourage former inmates to go back inside, not just the jail, but the Juvenile Detention Center, with a changed life. And, I am also working as a pastor for a congregation in Casper, Wyoming.

I even developed a good friendship with Lieutenant Clark. We didn't go swap spit or anything like that, but we were friends. Sadly, he ended up getting throat cancer and passed away. The jail asked if any of the Chaplains would speak at his funeral, and my hand went up. I realized that once again God had taken two adversaries and made them friends.

God also brought me into the prison. Wyoming medium security prison had been a target of mine for some time and God said no for five-years.

I never could understand why, but when He opened the door it was obvious. I had been preaching to guys that were headed into there for five-years and when I showed up, my reputation was already set. The church was already built.

CHAPTER 24
THE CRY OF MY HEART

In Mark 10:46-52, there is a story I deeply relate to in my own life. It was when Jesus was just leaving Jericho, He ran into a large crowd where Bart, a blind beggar, was sitting by the road. When he heard that it was Jesus of Nazareth, he began to cry out:

"'Jesus, Son of David, have mercy on me!' Many warned him to keep quiet, but he was crying out all the more, 'Have mercy on me, Son of David!' Jesus stopped and said, 'Call him.' So they called the blind man and said to him, "Have courage! Get up; He's calling for you.' He threw off his coat, jumped up, and came to Jesus. Then Jesus answered him, 'What do you want Me to do for you?' 'Teacher', the blind man said to Him, 'I want to see.' Jesus said to him, 'Go, your faith has saved you.' Immediately, he could see and began to follow Jesus on the road."

When I read this story, I hear Blind "Bert".

I was blind in my outlaw life. My heart was dead and empty.

Just like "Bart", Jesus spoke to me, and, in a blinding flash of light from His cross, He broke my heart open... and I could see again!

And, so, I threw off my colors and ran to Jesus. And have followed Him along this road ever since.

Without the Father, there was only darkness; without Christ, there was no life; without the Holy Spirit, there was no love. In this dark world, there is only One light. This light is for all of mankind. It is He who opens the eyes of the blind to see. The Lord Jesus Christ is that beacon.

AND, while the journey we have been on in this book is coming to a close, your journey is only beginning. You have not picked up this book by chance, but by fate. I have deeply prayed for every single person that will ever pick up this book. God has a destiny in mind for you.

If you are willing to lay down your own hard-heart and let Jesus in, when you stop fighting, and talk to Him, you will find the peace you've always been chasing after in everything, *but* God.

He will stop the screaming little child inside, trapped by all the hate.

And He will give you peace.

Sure, you may be a little bit of a mess, but God is looking at what you will become, not what you've been.

So, whether you're an outlaw,

a druggie,

a prisoner,

a cop,

or a pagan,

God can make the impossible become real.

He can heal the unhealable, and change the unchangeable.

My life is undeniable proof that there are no walls too high that God cannot reach over. There is no tomb too deep that He cannot reach down and lift you out of. There is no person that can stop you.

Just talk to Jesus, and He will make a way.

2 Corinthians 5:17 "Therefore, if anyone is in Christ, the new creation has come: The old is gone, The new is here."

-Pastor Bert Eldredge

GLOSSARY

25

Glossary of Terms

1) M/C (Motorcycle Club)

2) OutDweller (Nordic term for Outlaw the name of my club)

3) Prospect (Prospective member or unproven brother)

4) Patch holder (Full Member, but non-officer)

5) Sergeant at Arms (Club security, an enforcer)

6) Packing (You have a weapon)

7) Colors or a cut (Club logo, name, rockers on a vest)

8) Rockers Name and location of the club or territory in which they own

9) Celly (Your Cell mate)

10) Hemmed up (Locked up)

11) AB (Arian Brother aka White guy)

12) POD (Place Of Detention)

13) Ink (Tattoo's)

14) 1%er (Full blown outlaw biker with large groups and clout)

Definition of Love: To fully pour oneself into another without expectation of return affection. To surrender the desire to fulfill one's own needs in order to give another their heart' desire. (Bert's definition)

Definition of Use: To give in order to receive. To have an exchange of commerce whether it be sex, goods, emotions or services, only giving for the exchange of what you get. (Bert's definition)

UNDERSTANDING the hierarchy of a club is just like understanding your local lodge or your company. You have presidents and vice-presidents. You may get to a point of Nationals, which means they are officers over local chapter or state officers.

PRISON AND JAILS are very similar for their talk and descriptions and most folks have heard these in movies and books.

PICTURES

FAMILY

Bert, Kristie, Keshia

Kristie

Bert

BIKES

Kristie

Bert

Kristie

Wolfman

Kristie

Hombre de Sombra

Bert, Trenton

Bert

CLUB

The Original Brotherhood

Shovel Races

Nomad Norman, Keg Push

Bert, Keshia: Ring Toss

Bert, Keshia: True "Drag" Racing

Arizona Snowshoe

MINISTRY

Bert's Baptism

Kristie's Baptism

Maasai

Tribal Leader

Maasai Accepting Christ

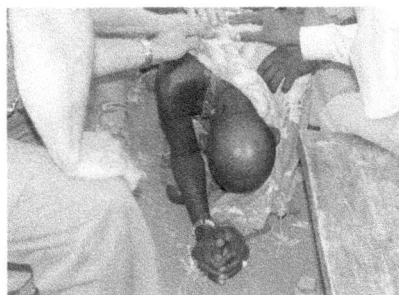

Maasai Born Again

Daniel Local Pastor

Church in the African Bush

ABOUT THE AUTHOR

Bert Eldredge

"I am a sheep in wolf's clothing going amongst the wolves to show the love of Christ." -Bert Eldredge

Pastor Bert Eldredge spent almost 30 years in M/C clubs. He spent 10 of those as the founder and president of the OutDwellers M/C. He now holds a Doctorate in Theology. He preaches and teaches in jails, prisons, schools, and wherever he is called.

www.ingramcontent.com/pod-product-compliance
Lightning Source LLC
LaVergne TN
LVHW041156080426
835511LV00006B/632